LONE PARENTHOOD

For Mariann, Amy and Lucy

LONE PARENTHOOD
Coping with constraints and making opportunities

edited by

Michael Hardey
University of Surrey

Graham Crow
University of Southampton

 **HARVESTER WHEATSHEAF**

New York   London   Toronto   Sydney   Tokyo   Singapore

First published 1991 by
Harvester Wheatsheaf,
66 Wood Lane End, Hemel Hempstead,
Hertfordshire, HP2 4RG
A division of
Simon & Schuster International Group

Typeset in 10/12 pt Palatino
by Keyset Composition, Colchester

Printed and bound in Great Britain by
Billing and Sons Limited, Worcester

British Library Cataloguing in Publication Data

Lone parenthood: Coping with constraints and
making opportunities.
I. Hardey, Michael   II. Crow, Graham
306.85

ISBN 0-7450-0964-6
ISBN 0-7450-0965-4 pbk

---

1 2 3 4 5 95 94 93 92 91

Contents

Acknowledgements

We would like to thank our colleagues at the Universities of Surrey and Southampton for their encouragement and support in the production of this book. We have also received constructive comments and criticism from a number of other people, especially those who participated in the Family Life in Lone-Parent Households conference at Surrey University. We would also like to thank Clare Grist and Martin Klopstock at Harvester Wheatsheaf for their assistance in all the stages of the production of this book.

Notes on the contributors

John Baker teaches in the Department of Social Policy and Professional Studies at the University of Hull. His previous publications include *The Neighbourhood Advice Centre* (1978).

Stephen Collins teaches Applied Social Studies at Bradford University. His previous publications include *Step-Parents and their Children* (1988) and he is currently working on historical representations of remarriage.

Graham Crow has taught Sociology at the University of Southampton since 1983. He has previously co-edited a collection of essays on domestic life, *Home and Family* (1989).

Maggie French teaches at the University of Maryland and the University of Essex. She has recently undertaken research into marriage and is currently working on transport policy.

Judith Glover teaches in the Sociology and Social Administration Department at Roehampton Institute of Higher Education. Her research interests include women's employment in Britain and France and the relationship between employment and domestic characteristics.

Michael Hardey researches and teaches at the University of Surrey. His work has involved research about lone-parent families and social policy. He is also engaged on a study of the organisation of health care.

John Haskey is a statistician working at the Office of Population Censuses and Surveys (OPCS). He has written widely on a number of topics including marriage and divorce, one-parent families, cohabitation, and ethnic minority populations

Gill Jones is a Research Fellow at the Centre for Educational Sociology, University of Edinburgh. Her recent research has focused on young people's transition to adulthood.

Jennie Popay is Senior Research Officer at Thomas Coram Research Unit at the University of London Institute of Education. She has previously written about lone parents as a co-author of *One Parent Families: Parents, children and public policy* (1983).

Sandra Shaw teaches Sociology at the University of Sheffield, where she is also completing her PhD thesis on lone mothers and divorce.

1 Introduction

Michael Hardey and Graham Crow

In broad terms, lone parents occupy a marginal position in contemporary British society. Their marginalisation is most immediately apparent when their disadvantaged economic position is considered, since the majority of lone parents have to manage their lives on incomes which need to be stretched to cover basic requirements. As a result, the connection between lone parenthood and poverty constitutes a profound challenge to social policy (Millar, 1989; Oppenheim, 1990). Lone parents' low incomes are closely linked to poor standards of housing, which may be marginal in a spatial sense as well, and to poor health for both themselves and their children, as the chapters by Crow and Hardey and Popay and Jones in this volume (Chapters 3 and 4) seek to demonstrate. In addition lone parents occupy a marginal position in social life more generally, being effectively excluded from full participation in mainstream activities not only by their lack of income but also by the couple-centred 'family' ideology which permeates the social structure (Allan, 1985; Elliot, 1986; Mullan, 1984). In a range of situations, from formal work organisations and official bureaucracies through to informal patterns of sociability and leisure opportunities, lone parenthood is not granted an equal status to the cultural norm of coupledom. In sum, lone parents tend to be distinctly poor in an affluent society, and noticeably isolated and alone in a generally couple-centred culture.

Lone parenthood is not only a set of constraints, however. In response to their situation, lone parents have developed a number of ways of dealing more or less well with economic and social marginalisation. These 'coping strategies' (Graham, 1984, 1987a, 1987b) are crucial means by which the best can be made of limited resources, allowing the creation of opportunities within constraints. Such strategies may make possible, for example, the

1

fulfilment of both employment and daycare responsibilities, which is the subject of Hardey and Glover's chapter in this volume (Chapter 5). Other chapters are also mindful of the need to break from the tradition of analysis which, despite often laudable intentions, tends to present lone parents as powerless victims of social disadvantage and by doing so to reinforce the stereotypical image of lone parents as dependent.

It is of course correct to observe, as Burgoyne has, that there is 'little that you as an individual can do to fight an economic and political system which treats one-parent families so shamefully' (1984, pp. 69–70), but the idea that lone parents respond submissively or fatalistically to their situation lacks supporting evidence. On the contrary, research has shown how lone parenthood requires that constraints are coped with (Cashmore, 1985), and through making the most of the limited economic and social opportunities open to them lone parents refute the charge of dependency and inadequacy which is frequently levelled against them. It remains the case that one-parent families 'are an unpopular group of whose difficulties the public is largely unaware' (Bramall, 1975, p. 152), and against this background it is easy for lone parents who are poor to be mistakenly perceived as 'poor parents', just as lone parents are also especially vulnerable to the conflation of 'families with problems' and 'problem families'.

The contributions to this volume are linked in other ways besides their acknowledgement of lone parents' marginality and their rejection of the dependent-lone-parent stereotype. To begin with, there is a recognition that it is necessary to approach lone parents and their children as households and families in their own right, and not as a mutant form of the so-called 'normal' two-parent family. Unless belief in the cultural 'normality' of the two-parent family is suspended, lone-parent families are condemned to unfavourable comparison. This ties in with the second linking theme of the book, that of stressing the diversity of lone-parent households. The growth in numbers of lone parents in recent years has been nothing short of dramatic, as Haskey's extensive research (reported in this volume and elsewhere) demonstrates. Equally striking is the heterogeneity to be found among lone parents, in terms of their routes into lone parenthood, the range of their material situations and the variety of personal experiences of lone parenthood. In consequence, generalisation about lone parents is something which requires a good deal of caution.

A third thread running through the chapters which follow is an awareness of the uncertainties surrounding lone parenthood. The doubts and conflicts experienced by lone parents reflect the competing and often contradictory pressures to which they are subject, bearing out Oakley's view that their social situation is 'full of ambiguities' (1974, p. 70). Such ambiguities are compounded by the fact that the constraints within which lone parents live are not static but dynamic, and the changing fortunes of lone parents in the fields of social policy (in particular the benefits system), the labour and housing markets, and in social relations more generally constitute a fourth focus of this collection. The overall picture of lone parenthood which emerges is one of resilience and inventiveness as well as unrelieved responsibilities and frustration in the face of adverse economic and social processes of marginalisation.

A VARIANT FAMILY FORM?

In his discussion of the question of whether one-parent families are more appropriately seen as a variant rather than a deviant family form, Chester (1977a) argued that the omens for lone parents, and especially for lone mothers, were broadly favourable. Chester took the growth in the numbers of one-parent families, together with shifts in thinking on the part of both policy-makers and society more generally, as reasons to anticipate the gradual reduction in economic difficulties and social stigma experienced by lone parents. There were, he concluded,

indications in England that the situation for one-parent families in general, and female-headed families in particular, is improving. . . . Social attitudes show signs of changing, and public policy has begun to modify the exclusive preference it has always shown for one particular form of married and family living. Despite such trends, however, there is far to go before the one-parent family could be said to be normalized, accepted and supported as an alternative to domestic orthodoxy (1977a, p. 160).

The position adopted by Chester may be characterised as one of cautious liberal optimism. It stands somewhat uneasily between the older, entrenched tradition of thought which sees in lone parenthood only the social problem of family 'failure' (Lewis, 1986) and the more recent, bolder assertions of lone-parent identity (Itzin, 1980).

There is no doubt that lone parents have been subject to a long history of stigmatisation, going back several centuries, for their 'deviance' from the two-parent norm (Macintyre, 1977; Page, 1984). In particular, critical attention has focused on women who have children without being married, who have borne a number of negative labels. 'Unmarried mothers', 'unwed mothers', 'unsupported mothers', 'fatherless families' and 'incomplete families' are terms which identify their subjects by what they are not (that is, parents in couples) rather than by what they are. Other terminology has combined more open hostility with coy euphemism. Bowlby and his followers, for example, warned of the 'delinquency' of the 'problem family', and identified the mother of an illegitimate child as 'pathologically disturbed' (Riley, 1983).

Efforts by more sympathetic participants in this debate to rename their subject have been important in steering the discussion into the use of less evaluative terminology. The term 'unmarried mothers' gave way to the broader category of 'one-parent families' only relatively recently, as the presence of common characteristics among all lone parents, whatever their routes into lone parenthood, became more widely recognised, and here the 1970s stand as something of a watershed. This decade saw publication of the Finer Report on one-parent families (DHSS, 1974), while the previous year the National Council for the Unmarried Mother and Her Child had changed its name to the National Council for One Parent Families (Bramall, 1975). Chester's proposition that one-parent families are in a process of transition from 'deviant' to 'variant' status also dates from this period. In turn, the term 'one-parent families' has been objected to because of its tendency to play down the plight of single mothers, for whom 'an overwhelming factor in their situation is lack of a male wage' (Pascall, 1986, p. 4). The term 'lone-parent household' goes only some way towards meeting this criticism, and it has to be recognised that there is no universal agreement in this area, where the categories in use continue to evolve rapidly (Crow and Hardey, 1991). The contributions to this volume reflect the diversity of terminology currently surrounding lone parenthood as writers strive to avoid the pitfalls of the past relating to misleading and judgemental language.

It is certainly the case that lone parents have become more 'normal' in modern British society in a straightforward numerical sense. Haskey's chapter in this volume (Chapter 2) charts the continued rise in the number of lone parents to the point at which there are over a million one-parent families, which make up 15 per cent of all families containing dependent children. The proportions of parents and children passing through life in a one-parent family can only be approximated, but given that lone parenthood is a status which has high rates of movement in and out, the figures would undoubtedly be high (Nissel, 1987; Rimmer, 1983), moving towards a situation where it will be perhaps as high as one in four. The great change in recent years is, as Haskey's chapter shows, in the growth in the number of marriages ending in separation and divorce, but it is also important to note the growth in the numbers of mothers who have never married. With 27 per cent of live births in 1989 to single mothers, even allowing for half of this group being accounted for by cohabitation this still leaves a significant new trend, reflecting the 'diminished stigma of illegitimacy' (Nissel, 1987, p. 228) along with the ending of legal discrimination.

In some quarters attention is thus focusing once again on particular groups of lone parents rather than on lone parents as a whole. A recent volume on 'variant family forms' highlighted the position of 'never-married, single, adolescent parents' (Chilman, 1988) rather than lone parents overall. The situation of these young mothers can be seen to be particularly vulnerable when it is compared to the less disadvantaged position of widows and divorcees, with whom they may have relatively little in common. From another perspective, never-married mothers may be portrayed as different from other lone parents to the extent that they have positively chosen motherhood outside marriage, as clearly some have (Renvoize, 1985). The latter chapters in this volume deal mainly with lone parents who head a 'variant family form' by virtue of having left a two-parent situation; thus the different research projects reported on in the chapters by French, Shaw and Collins (Chapters 7, 8, 9) were conducted exclusively among formerly married lone mothers. Where in other chapters never-married mothers are considered alongside separated and divorced lone parents, the impression arises of an important divergence in their experiences. This is also the case for lone fathers, who tend to be socially invisible and whose particular circumstances have been relatively neglected in research.

It would, of course, be a mistake to overlook the things lone-parent households have in common, most notably the probability of poorer housing, poorer health and lower incomes than are found among two-parent households, and to this extent they 'deviate' collectively from the norm of the wider society. There is, however, a marked absence of a shared identity among lone parents, who are likely to be as conscious of the differences that exist between them as they are of their common situation. For this reason alone Chester's idea of the one-parent family as a variant family form is questionable, since it is at least arguable that one-parent families constitute a variety of alternatives rather than a single one.

In addition, the idea of one-parent families' 'variation' is insufficiently critical of its norm, as Burgoyne noted in her assessment of the writings of Chester and other family sociologists: 'the power and continuing saliency of typifications of the nuclear family as the only normal, natural or even healthy context in which to live and raise children continues to act as a deterrent to the widespread acceptance of alternatives to the conventional family' (1987, p. 86). Burgoyne's own work on remarriage (Burgoyne and Clark, 1984) highlights the differences between step-families and marriage first time round, and raises doubts about the idea of lumping together all households in which there are two parents and dependent children. The necessary difference of step-families, despite their attempts to re-create 'normal' family life, is a theme pursued in Collins's chapter in this volume (Chapter 9).

Rather than attempting to answer the question of whether the one-parent family is a 'variant' rather than a 'deviant' form of the conventional family, it may be more fruitful to abandon such efforts and instead to follow Gittins's more historically informed injunction to 'start thinking of *families* rather than the family' (1985, p. 2; original emphasis). In other words, there is much to commend the suggestion that reference should be made 'to "all types of families" to avoid the implication that there is only one "normal" type' (Genovese, 1984, p. 6; see also Bernardes, 1985; Morgan, 1985), noting in the process that one-parent families are prominent among these types. Such an approach allows reference to be made to one-parent families (or lone-parent households) in the plural, as a mark of recognition not only of their difference from other family and household types but also of their internal diversity. It also avoids the biological reductionism of the traditional model of the 'family' (Barrett and McIntosh, 1982).

THE DIVERSITY OF LONE-PARENT HOUSEHOLDS

All lone parents have responsibility for bringing up their children without the presence of a partner in the household, and as a result they necessarily share certain common characteristics and interests. These common interests were taken to be significant enough to justify the adoption of a broad campaigning platform by the National Council for One Parent Families, pushing for a reorganisation of social policy so that discrimination between different types of lone parents gave way to access to similar provision for all lone parents (Bramall, 1975). This project has encountered the predictable obstacle of restraint in public spending, the established tendency 'to adapt our social conscience to the public purse' (Yudkin and Holme, 1963, p. 68), but it has also been less effective in bringing about the anticipated improvement in lone parents' position for other reasons too. Prominent among these other reasons are the continuing diversity of lone parents' experiences and the resultant limitation of their collective strength (Crow and Hardey, 1991).

The diversity of lone-parent households has several dimensions. To begin with, lone parents may be differentiated according to their routes into lone parenthood, ranging 'from the young unmarried mother, through the separated and divorced to the middle-aged widow' (O'Higgins *et al.*, 1988, p. 232), and also including lone fathers. The majority of lone parents in modern Britain are lone mothers who have become so through the processes of separation and divorce, with single (never-married) mothers the next most important group in numerical terms, and widows and lone fathers making up relatively small groups by comparison. Haskey's chapter in this volume explores the demographic differences to be found between these groups of lone parents, bringing out the presence of quite distinct profiles relating to age and number of dependent children. He also shows that the relative significance of each group of lone parents has changed quite dramatically in recent years, noting in particular the growth of young single mothers, a group who in the past would have been under greater pressure to give up their babies for adoption (Hartmann, 1987; Macintyre, 1977).

There are conflicting perspectives on how far such trends represent a change in lone parenthood being actively chosen by the individuals concerned. Renvoize's study of women deliberately becoming single mothers found it to be a growing phenomenon but still 'primarily a middle-class choice' (1985, p. 19). Leonard and Speakman suggest that for lesbians, becoming single mothers by choice is 'a very significant step forward in forming their identity' (1986, p. 60), although estimating numbers in this group is clearly problematic. The teenage mothers in Phoenix's study were more ambivalent about lone motherhood, although 'More than a quarter of those asked in late pregnancy about advantages and disadvantages of marriage were unequivocally negative about marriage, seeing it as having only disadvantages for women' (1991, p. 107). Despite the growth in their numbers over recent years, however, single mothers by choice remain a minority among lone parents as a whole (Cashmore, 1985; Close, 1985), and a distinct minority by virtue of their never having been married.

The existence of several routes into lone parenthood matters, not least because the way in which individuals become lone parents has a strong bearing on their subsequent fortunes. When considering the position of lone-parent households in the housing market, in terms of their tenure and the material standard of their accommodation, the picture is an uneven one, as Crow and Hardey's chapter shows. There is a greater likelihood of owner-occupation among widows and lone fathers, while single mothers are located in the most vulnerable circumstances. This variation in housing-market position is part of the explanation offered by Popay and Jones in their chapter, which explores the diverse patterns of health and illness to be found among lone-parent families. Routes into lone parenthood also have an influence on individuals' ability to take up employment opportunities, since this is determined to no small degree by the ages of dependent children and the availability of daycare. Hardey and Glover's chapter contains a number of illustrations of how different routes into lone parenthood affect the types of material constraints on their ability to enter paid work, while French's chapter demonstrates that divorce does not necessarily rule out former partners undertaking daycare in order that lone mothers may earn an income.

The diversity to be found among lone-parent households also has an international dimension. Baker's chapter in this volume (Chapter 6) observes that although there is a recognisable long-term trend in all the countries of Western Europe for the number of lone parents to rise, there are significant differences between these countries in terms of how far this process has developed. It may be noted that the growth in lone-parent numbers has gone further still in other countries such as the United States (Chilman, 1988). It may also be seen that these international differences are linked into contrasting patterns of welfare provision and economic opportunities. Baker's chapter concentrates on the illuminating contrast of anti-poverty strategies as they relate to Britain and France, but the point about there being international diversity in the policies adopted towards lone parents has a broader validity (Wicks, 1983); certainly the situation is different again in the United States (Morris, 1990).

A further element in the diversity of lone parents concerns the length of time over which lone parenthood is experienced. Ermisch has shown that single mothers are likely to be lone parents for a significantly shorter period than are lone mothers whose marriages ended, and a divorced mother's prospects of remarriage depend, he argues, 'on her age, educational attainments, her experience in paid employment and the size of her family' (1989, p. 53). Also of great importance here – albeit more difficult to quantify – is the experience of marriage which she brings with her. Shaw's chapter in this volume is critical of the assumption that women who have been lone mothers for long periods have somehow 'failed' in their efforts to find a new partner, proposing instead that they may have positively rejected the option of remarriage. Her research findings echo Hartmann's

(1987) argument that many women may prefer lone parenthood to marriage, because although lone parenthood is linked to poverty, it is also associated with greater autonomy and less housework than conventional marriage entails. Collins's chapter on the conflicting pressures to which lone parents are subject provides further reasons why it is mistaken to think of remarriage as necessarily an attractive solution to the difficulties of lone parenthood, even if it is one ultimately taken by the majority of lone parents, encouraged to do so by friends, family and professional advisers (Burgoyne *et al.*, 1987).

UNCERTAINTIES AND AMBIGUITIES IN THE EXPERIENCE OF LONE PARENTHOOD

It is unsurprising to find lone parents expressing mixed feelings about their lives, since they are subject to competing and often contradictory pressures. Lone parents are expected to 'cope' with their situation even though the resources available for them to do this with are generally inadequate; in consequence, caring for their children's well-being may be at the expense of their own (Graham, 1984). Similarly the roles of parent and worker may come into conflict, without any obvious means of resolution, so that lone parents find themselves pulled in two different directions (Land, 1983). There is also a tension to be found in whether the status of 'lone parent' is treated as a positive and long-term identity or regarded more negatively as a short-term, transitional phase prior to cohabitation, marriage or remarriage. For all these reasons, there is much ambiguity surrounding lone parenthood in contemporary society (Kamerman and Kahn, 1988).

The uncertain position of lone parents is revealed when the basic matter of their sources of income is considered. It has been observed that 'Historically the modern state has experienced considerable difficulty in deciding whether to treat lone mothers as workers or mothers' (Lewis, 1989, p. 595), and the current policy moves to encourage greater labour-market participation by lone mothers do contrast sharply with the emphasis placed on the dangers of mother–child separation during earlier postwar decades. A rather different set of priorities surrounds lone fatherhood, though the conflicting demands of work and daycare make it too a 'problematic status' (Hipgrave, 1982). Of course, all parents who attempt to combine daycare and employment face the task of 'juggling' (Brannen and Moss, 1988; Furstenberg *et al.*, 1987) their various responsibilities, performing the 'balancing act between work and home' (Crehan, 1986, p. 31), but lone parents do so in the more stressful circumstances of the absence of a partner. As Hardey and Glover argue, this situation reveals the underdeveloped nature of daycare provision in modern Britain and helps to account for the comparatively low levels of employment among lone parents, while Baker's chapter shows what can be learnt from the French policy of enabling lone parents to take up job opportunities. In Britain, the absence of appropriate provision means that much more onus is placed on lone parents' ability to develop individual strategies for coping with the competing demands of employers and children.

It is not only in their attempts to combine daycare and employment that lone parents encounter difficulties which are also confronted by parents in couples. Boulton's study of women with pre-school children excluded lone mothers, but reported the range of feelings about daycare, 'from frustration, irritation and boredom to delight, pleasure and enjoyment' (1983, p. 53), which are also experienced (and, arguably, experienced more intensely) by lone parents. The chapters by French, Shaw and Collins illustrate in different ways the heightened sense of achievement which raising children single-handedly brings to lone parents, while at the same time inducing feelings of guilt about the adequacy of their parenting and feelings of frustration at the unrelieved nature of their daycare responsibilities. Similarly the chapter by Crow and Hardey highlights the conflicting pressures surrounding lone parents' attempts to secure a safe, comfortable and affordable home for themselves and their children which is also close to work opportunities and informal networks of support.

Although lone parents are likely to be economically disadvantaged, there is also a growing literature which suggests that considerable numbers of them come to value various aspects of life outside a two-parent household. In a straightforward financial sense, separated or divorced lone mothers may paradoxically be 'better off poorer' (Graham, 1987a, p. 59; Hartmann, 1987) where lone parenthood allows them greater control over the household's resources, while the greater autonomy and control over their time which a lone parent enjoys following the departure of a former partner may lead to a feeling of being 'happier alone' (Sharpe, 1984, p. 205) and a sense of relief from the pressures of marital disagreements (Gordon, 1990). Shaw's chapter confirms the presence of such positive aspects of lone parenthood alongside the more negative ones relating to financial anxieties and loneliness, although it is open to debate whether these experiences justify Itzin's description of *Splitting Up* as 'liberating' (1980, p. 2).

The balance of positive and negative experiences of lone parenthood is subject to a good deal of change as time passes. In Arendell's study, divorce presented mothers with legal, economic and social dilemmas which required a lengthy period of adjustment. Most of her respondents

struggled for years to attain a satisfactory personal and social identity. In one sense they were now single; divorce had ended their married status. In another sense they were not single; they were mothers who were no longer married. The cultural definitions of these two identities – single woman and primary parent – were often contradictory, and these women found no traditions to guide them in their efforts to integrate conflicting roles (1986, p. 128).

In other words, it is impossible to specify an unambiguous set of defining characteristics of lone-parent identity, nor is it possible to point to a precise moment at which an individual adopts such an identity. It is rather the case that a process of becoming a lone parent is involved, a theme explored in French's chapter on the various stages of adjustment to lone parenthood. Over time the experience of coping alone and managing to deal with the various demands which the situation throws up allows a more positive identity to emerge, but the earlier stages of coming to terms with lone parenthood represent a lengthy period of adjustment during which the hardships can seem overwhelming.

The economic factors behind the probability that lone parents will leave lone parenthood by getting married or remarried are undoubtedly substantial (Ermisch, 1989). The 'price' of the greater autonomy reported by lone parents includes the likelihood of poverty and poor housing conditions, and the pressures to leave lone parenthood by entering a new couple-based relationship are concomitantly strong. The decision to remarry or cohabit is by no means straightforwardly economic, however, since the role of ideology is also powerful in these circumstances. Collins argues in his chapter that the cultural norm of two-parent families is very hard to resist, although Shaw's research indicates that the experiences of lone parenthood make an individual wary of returning to a marital relationship similar to the one they have left, just as widows may find the idea of a 'replacement partner' difficult to adjust to. Preparedness to give up lone parenthood for remarriage is some way short of universal.

SOCIAL CHANGE, SOCIAL POLICY AND CHANGING FORTUNES

Historical comparisons suggest that while the position of lone-parent households has been transformed in many ways, in other respects there are very powerful continuities. Haskey's chapter charts the dramatic shifts that have taken place in the numbers and demographic characteristics of lone parents, while Hardey and Glover's chapter brings out the importance of the growth of their employment opportunities. Against this, the evidence presented by Crow and Hardey and Popay and Jones that lone-parent households face poorer standards of housing and health than their two-parent counterparts suggests that they remain a structurally disadvantaged group whose relative position has not improved significantly despite repeated social policy reforms. In sum, 'lone-parent families are a growing group that is important to policy, not least because typically they have relatively few resources in relation to their needs' (O'Higgins *et al.*, 1988, p. 231).

The Finer Report (DHSS, 1974) did much to stimulate the hopes of many observers that social policies relating to one-parent families were subject to a long-term process of liberalisation, and that the peculiar disadvantages to which lone parents were subject would be systematically eroded. Such hopes have proved unfounded, since the Finer Report's own recommendations foundered, as previous reform programmes had, on the twin objections of undue cost and the 'unfairness' to two-parent families of singling out one-parent families for supposedly preferential treatment (Deacon and Bradshaw, 1983). Baker's chapter in this volume argues that there is a good deal of economic sense in considering alternative anti-poverty strategies such as those adopted in France, where a range of measures empower lone parents in the labour market and have the overall effect of reducing their dependence on the state. The reluctance on the part of British policy-makers to experiment with such initiatives suggests that reformers face not only the obstacle of non-interventionist economic philosophy but also the barrier of conventional familial ideology, the assumption 'that people not only do live in nuclear families but ought to do so' (Abbott and Wallace, 1989, p. 87). At the hands of these ideologists, lone-parent families are 'presented as culpably deviant scroungers' (Cook, 1989, p. 16; see also Squires, 1990).

Against such a background it is perhaps unsurprising to find that lone-parent households are becoming more rather than less distinct in contemporary society, caught in the downward pressures which the process of social polarisation entails (Townsend *et al.*, 1987). Lone mothers are especially vulnerable to these pressures given the disadvantaged position of women in the labour market and the more general 'feminization of poverty' (Glendinning and Millar, 1987; Townsend *et al.*, 1987). The process of social polarisation poses a particular problem in housing, where lone-parent households are increasingly likely to find themselves in the 'residual' parts of the housing market, as Crow and Hardey's chapter shows. It is in the inner cities and the run-down outer estates that the most vulnerable lone parents, the 'group of single mothers dependent on welfare for very long periods of time' (Field, 1989, p. 5), are disproportionately concentrated.

The seriousness of the problem of lone parents being locked into the poorer parts of cities is demonstrated by their inclusion in the list of characteristics used by the Archbishop of Canterbury's Commission to identify 'Urban Priority Areas'. In the Commission's report, *Faith in the City* (1985), deprived areas are defined in terms of high numbers of single-parent families, ethnic minority families and old people living alone, together with unemployment, overcrowding, and homes lacking basic amenities. The overall picture painted of these areas is one of 'economic decline, physical decay and social disintegration' (1985, p. 24), and of growing isolation of their inhabitants from the rest of society. Haskey's chapter sheds further light on the link between lone parenthood and ethnicity which these broad impressions suggest by demonstrating the diversity that is to be found among different ethnic minority groups in relation to lone parenthood. Almost a quarter of West Indian households are made up of one-parent families, while in contrast the proportion of lone-parent households among Asian ethnic groups is similar to that of the white population. To the extent that lone parents and ethnic minority populations are located together in poorer parts of cities, it is the result of their shared poverty rather than because of any more direct connection put forward by writers of the 'black underclass' school (Segalman and Marsland, 1989).

There are essentially three possible routes out of poverty open to lone parents. The first is an unlikely prospect, since it involves a commitment by the state to increased welfare payments to a group whose numbers have grown dramatically in recent years and look set to continue to rise. The solution of lone-parent households' poverty by means of increased benefits faces a host of obstacles, not only those relating to cost but also others concerned with the mechanics of delivering the payments. If the idea of a benefit payable to all lone parents at a level high enough to make an impact on their poverty is objected to on the grounds of prohibitive cost, as inevitably it is, the alternative approach adopting means testing is also fraught with difficulties. It is possible for means-tested schemes of assistance to be adapted to the special situation of lone parents to some extent (Berthoud *et al.*, 1981; Weale *et al.*, 1984). Even if the difficulties of low take-up of benefits and complicated assessment procedures to determine eligibility can be overcome (Townsend *et al.*, 1987), however, such measures remain an attempt to add something on to low incomes rather than offering an escape route from poverty to economic sufficiency and independence.

In addition it is necessary to mention what is perhaps the biggest obstacle of all to the creation of a welfare payment route out of poverty for lone parents – that is, their relative unpopularity with voters and their representatives in Parliament (Whiteley and Winyard, 1987). New legislation based on the White Paper *Children Come First* (HMSO, 1990) which is intended to increase the proportion of lone parents' incomes coming from maintenance payments is in this context a superficially attractive option. This approach places greater emphasis upon parental responsibilities of former partners, but in general their incomes are inadequate to cover the costs of maintaining two households. In consequence this legislation is unlikely to change the situation where only a small minority of lone parents have maintenance payments as their main source of income, while the majority receive no maintenance at all (Millar, 1989).

The second route out of poverty for lone parents is via employment, and this option has been more actively pursued in recent years. The Finer Report (DHSS, 1974) had argued strongly that lone parents should be given the choice of whether or not to take up paid work, and employment can be an important route to greater financial independence for many. The financial reasons behind lone parents taking up paid work are supplemented by social reasons, such as the opportunities to mix with other adults in the workplace. Such non-financial benefits of employment may apply even where taking a job incurs economic costs, as has been indicated by the research which found that one in eight lone mothers on Family Income Supplement (the forerunner of Family Credit) 'opted to work rather than receive a higher income through SB [Supplementary Benefit, the forerunner of Income Support]' (Fuller and Stevenson, 1983, p. 30). The demoralising effects of long-term dependence on benefits, together with the positive attractions of social contacts made through work, predispose lone parents to take up employment, but this is not always a viable course of action, as Hardey and Glover's chapter shows. The limited availability of some form of inexpensive daycare is arguably the single most important obstacle to lone parents seeking employment. In the absence of adequate systems of daycare and other support to enable them to take up employment opportunities, divorced mothers will 'continue to experience a conflict between their family responsibilities and paid employment for a considerable period after their marriage has ended' (Land, 1983, p. 81).

The third option for lone parents seeking to escape poverty is the course of leaving lone parenthood and entering into new household arrangements through cohabitation, marriage or remarriage. The economic pressures on them to follow this course are undoubtedly great, even though the implementation of social security rules about cohabitation still acts as an obstacle to the formation of long-term relationships (Brown, 1988; Marsden, 1973). According to Oppenheim (1990), the proportion of single parents living in poverty (defined as receiving less than half average income after housing costs) is 47 per cent, compared to 20 per cent of married couples with children; for single parents not in full-time work the proportion rises to 58 per cent. Lone parenthood provides a good example of how women's welfare is structured around their fortunes in 'the labour-market and the marriage-market' (Groves, 1983, p. 60). There is, however, an important proviso relating to the fact that there may be significant inequalities within households (Brannen and Wilson, 1987; Pahl, 1989), and the implication that remarriage may disguise rather than overcome poverty. Concern about this outcome and about the dangers of exchanging one form of dependence for another made the lone mothers reported on in Shaw's chapter wary of remarriage. It is also significant to note that ideological rather than material factors are given greater prominence in the explanation of the popularity of remarriage offered in Collins's chapter.

One of the central concerns of social policy in this area has been to avoid making lone parenthood an 'attractive' option. Used as a deterrent to lone parenthood, social policy must inevitably fail to prevent lone parents from falling into poverty, and thus comes into conflict with the objective of preventing child poverty. The ideology of the conventional nuclear family remains an enormously powerful one, despite the growth of household diversity over recent years. The 'assumed predominance of the nuclear family form' (Williams, 1989, p. 163) has had negative implications for unconventional households (such as lone-parent households) throughout the welfare system, particularly in the areas of income maintenance, housing and daycare; all these issues are addressed in the following chapters.

The growth of unconventional households has been responded to by policy-makers as 'a problem in itself rather than a new set of needs to be met' (Williams, 1989, p. 163). Baker's chapter argues that academics have unwittingly contributed to this situation by failing to become sufficiently engaged in public debate about the various policy options and about the position of lone parents in contemporary society more generally, although other writers suggest that policy-makers have a 'trained incapacity' (Mills, 1970) to utilise alternative paradigms. The methodological difficulties of researching and reporting on as heterogeneous a group as lone parents have undoubtedly played a part in bringing about this situation, but they are not insurmountable problems. The chapters which make up this volume represent the result of research undertaken from a range of methodological and disciplinary perspectives, but they are all concerned to draw out the links between what Mills, in his challenge to the academic community, called 'personal troubles' and 'public issues' (1970, p. 14). Lone parenthood is, after all, both a 'personal trouble' and a 'public issue'.

2 Lone parenthood and demographic change*

John Haskey

The large growth in the number of one-parent families has been a phenomenon of the postwar period, and of the last two decades in particular (Haskey, 1989a). The reasons for the growth may be seen in Figure 2.1, which shows the trends in divorce, births outside marriage, and new widowhoods and widowerhoods – events which are associated with the creation of one-parent families. Apart from the immediate aftermath of the Second World War – when the annual numbers of divorces and births outside marriage temporarily rose, but subsequently fell – general trends can be seen: a growth in the numbers of couples divorcing; a large increase in births outside marriage, especially since the mid 1970s; and a decline in new widowhoods and widowerhoods.

Figure 2.1, however, provides only a partial picture of the additional numbers of one-parent families coming into existence each year, for a number of reasons. For example, in the 1950s and 1960s births to single women were more likely than in recent years to lead to the parents marrying, or the child being offered for adoption. Also, not all married couples who separate ultimately divorce, so that some one-parent families come into existence through either an informal or a judicial separation, rather than by a divorce. Because of such considerations, it is necessary to be clear which families are to be included as one-parent families, before considering estimates of their numbers.

* This chapter was written by John Haskey, who is alone responsible for the opinions expressed, which are not necessarily those of OPCS.

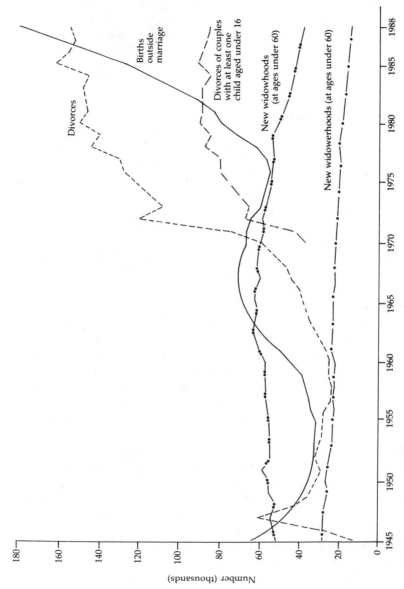

Figure 2.1 Trends in divorce, births outside marriage, and widow(er)hoods, 1945–89, England and Wales

DEFINITION OF A ONE-PARENT FAMILY

The definition of a one-parent family which is used for official, statistical purposes is the one adopted in the Finer Report on one-parent families, commissioned by the Department of Health and Social Security in 1969 (DHSS, 1974). The Report defined a one-parent family as 'a mother or a father living without a spouse (and not cohabiting) with his or her never-married dependent child or children aged either under 16, or from 16 to (under) 19 and undertaking full-time education'. This definition of one-parent families – which is used by the Department of Social Security – makes the task of estimating numbers difficult, since information on cohabitation is absent from the main sources of demographic data, and in particular from the census.

If estimating the number of one-parent families in existence at a particular time – the 'stock' – presents difficulties, so too does the estimation of the related 'flows' – that is, the various ways in which one-parent families come into and cease existence. The stock and flows can be represented diagrammatically as in Figure 2.2, where it may be seen that a family with one or more children may at some stages be classified as a one-parent family and at others as a two-parent family, depending upon the changes in the parents' – or indeed the children's – circumstances. Information on some of these changes is sparse or nonexistent; for example, the precise time at which a couple separate or start cohabiting. However, estimating the number of one-parent families existing at a certain time is rather more straightforward than trying to quantify the dynamics of how their numbers rise and fall.

ESTIMATED NUMBERS OF ONE-PARENT FAMILIES

In recent years, the number of one-parent families has been estimated afresh annually by comparing estimates using a number of different methods and data sources, and concluding a 'best estimate'. Table 2.1 gives the resulting 'best estimates' since 1984, and some earlier official estimates.

The number of one-parent families in Great Britain has increased considerably since the early 1970s, from around

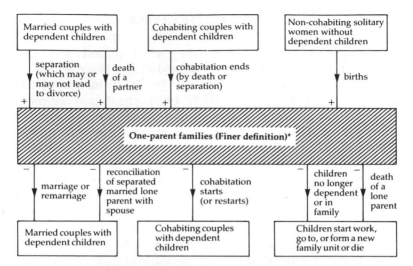

*The Finer definition of a one-parent family is a mother or father living without a spouse (and not cohabiting) with his or her never-married dependent child aged either under 16, or from 16 to (under) 19 and undertaking full-time education.

Note: A one-parent family may be created in any of the four ways indicated in the top half of the diagram; the same one-parent family can, with a few obvious exceptions, cease existence by *any* of the five routes shown in the lower half of the diagram. Dependent upon circumstances, lone parents and their dependent children can pass into and out of the stock of one-parent families more than once, as may be appreciated from the diagram.

Figure 2.2 One-parent families: Ways in which their numbers are increased and depleted

600,000 to just over one million – by more than 50 per cent. This growth in numbers has been common to most industrialised countries, although the largest increases have been reported in Great Britain, Australia and the United States; in other countries such as France, Japan and Switzerland, the increase in numbers

Table 2.1 Official estimates of the number of one-parent families, 1971–86, Great Britain

	Thousands				
Years	1971	1976	1984	1985	1986
Number of one-parent families	570	750	940	970	1010

has been 20 per cent or less (Duskin, 1988). However, for the majority of industrialised countries, the increase has ranged between 30 and 50 per cent (*ibid.*).

Table 2.2 gives the estimated numbers of the different categories of one-parent families in Great Britain, derived from the estimated total numbers of one-parent families in the same years. The largest percentage increases in numbers over the past ten years have occurred for single (never-married) lone mothers and divorced lone mothers. The number of widowed lone mothers actually fell by 30 per cent during the period. All these findings are consistent with the trends shown in Figure 2.1. Table 2.2 also shows – using results from the 1986–8 General Household Surveys (GHS) – that currently one in every eleven one-parent families is headed by a lone father, and over one in seven families with dependent children is a one-parent family. (A dependent child is defined as aged under sixteen or from sixteen to eighteen [inclusive] and in full-time education.)

TRENDS IN FAMILIES* WITH DEPENDENT CHILDREN

Figure 2.3 shows the trends in the proportion of all families with dependent children which are headed by a lone parent, distinguishing separately the proportions headed by lone fathers and lone mothers – and also the proportions by lone mothers of different marital statuses. In 1971, approximately one in thirteen, or 8 per cent, of all families with dependent children was a one-parent family, but this proportion steadily rose to 15 per cent – over one in seven – in 1987. Virtually all this increase is due to the growth in the proportion of lone mothers; since 1971, lone-father families have accounted for just over 1 per cent of all families with dependent children. Married-couple families with dependent children formed 85 per cent of all families with dependent children in 1987.

---

* In the remaining sections of this chapter – which deal with distributions of one-parent families, rather than estimates of their numbers – no adjustment has been made for the incidence of cohabitation among lone parents, but the effect of adjustment required would be negligible upon the statistics presented.

Table 2.2 Estimated numbers of one-parent families, 1971–86, Great Britain

Type of family with dependent children*	Numbers (thousands)				Percentage increase 1976–86	Percentages (from GHS 1986–88)	
	1971	1976	1985	1986			
Lone mothers							
Single	90	130	210	230	+77	26	3.8
Separated	170	185	180	190	+3	19	2.8
Divorced	120	230	400	410	+78	39	5.8
Widowed	120	115	90	80	−30	7	1.0
Lone mothers	500	660	880	910	+38	91	13.3
Lone fathers	70	90	90	100	+11	9	1.3
Lone parents	570	750	970	1010	+35	100	14.7
Married-couple families†							85.3
All families							100.0

*Dependent children are defined as aged under 16 or 16 to 18 and in full-time education.
†Includes some cohabiting couples.

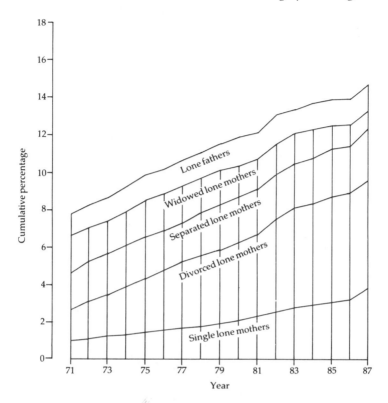

Three-year moving averages used (apart from 1971)

Figure 2.3 Percentage of all families with dependent children headed by lone mothers (by their marital status) and by lone fathers, 1971–88, Great Britain

Single and divorced lone-mother families have both formed growing proportions of all families with dependent children; together they formed 2.7 per cent in 1971, but 9.6 per cent in 1987. In contrast, the relative numbers of separated and widowed lone mothers have both declined slightly, so that together they formed 4.0 per cent of all families with dependent children in 1971, and 3.8 per cent in 1987.

The growth in the relative number of one-parent families headed by a single (never-married) mother is due to the increase in the proportion of all births which take place outside marriage.

This proportion reached 27 per cent in Great Britain in 1989, although approximately half these births were jointly registered by both mother and father, residing at the same address (Dollamore, 1990), and in these cases the family would not count as a one-parent family. Nevertheless, the proportion of all births which are outside marriage and either registered by the mother alone, or by both parents living at different addresses, has grown consistently (*ibid.*). The increase in the number of single lone mothers may also be partly due to a growth in the proportion of single mothers who bring up their children themselves – the number of children adopted has declined dramatically since 1971. In addition, perhaps because there is now less stigma than formerly in being a single mother, the proportion of single lone mothers who subsequently marry – whether they marry the child's father or not – has probably fallen.

Similarly, the rate of divorce increased substantially between 1971 and the 1980s; it then grew more slowly until 1985, when legislative changes led to an extra upward surge. (The divorce rate changed by approximately the same proportionate amount as occurred in the number of divorces, as shown in Figure 2.1.) In addition, the rate of remarriage amongst all divorced women has fallen steadily, and if the corresponding rate for divorced women with dependent children were to have fallen similarly, the number of divorced lone-mother families would be expected to have increased in number, through both the inflow increasing and the outflow decreasing. Widowed lone mothers now form a smaller part of all families with dependent children than they did at the beginning of the 1970s, not only because of the increase in numbers of single and divorced lone mothers but also because their numbers have actually declined, as Figure 2.1 and Table 2.2 reveal.

As well as considering the proportions lone mothers of the different marital statuses form of all families with dependent children, information is often needed on the proportions which lone mothers of the different marital statuses form of all lone mothers. These proportions are given in Table 2.3 for selected three-year periods.

Single and divorced lone mothers have both formed growing proportions of all lone mothers, whilst separated and widowed lone mothers have both declined as a proportion of all lone mothers. Currently, divorced lone mothers account for 43 per

Table 2.3 Distribution of one-parent families (percentages) by marital status of lone mother or lone father, 1971–88, Great Britain

Type of one-parent family with dependent children*	Years					Change: 1971–73 to 1986–88
	1971–73	1975–77	1979–81	1982–84	1986–88	
Lone mothers						
Single	17	17	20	23	28	+11
Separated	30	24	24	20	21	−9
Divorced	27	37	40	45	43	+16
Widowed	26	22	16	12	8	−18
Total – percentage	100	100	100	100	100	
sample no.	(1005)	(1237)	(1341)	(1260)	(1314)	
Lone fathers						
Single	4	2	2	5	5	+1
Separated	37	37	31	27	26	−11
Divorced	20	31	39	42	44	+24
Widowed	39	30	28	27	25	−14
Total – percentage	100	100	100	100	100	
– sample no.	(155)	(174)	(192)	(131)	(125)	
Lone mothers	86.3	87.1	87.2	90.4	91.0	+4.7
Lone fathers	13.7	12.9	12.8	9.6	9.0	−4.7
Total – percentage	100	100	100	100	100	
sample no.	(1165)	(1421)	(1538)	(1394)	(1444)	

*Dependent children are defined as aged under 16 or from 16 to 18 (inclusive) and in full-time education.
Source: General Household Surveys

cent of all lone mothers, single lone mothers for 28 per cent, separated lone mothers for 21 per cent and widowed lone mothers for 8 per cent.

Information is rarely provided on the marital status of lone fathers, mostly because, even in total, they form only a small part of all lone parents, and so, in sample surveys, the sample numbers of lone fathers in the different marital statuses are relatively quite small (Haskey, 1986). However, Table 2.3 analyses GHS results giving the distributions of lone fathers by their marital status, noting the somewhat small sample sizes on which they are based.

The profile by marital status of lone fathers is very different from that of lone mothers; a much higher proportion of lone fathers are widowed and a much smaller proportion are single, although divorced and separated lone fathers form roughly similar proportions of all lone fathers as their lone-mother counterparts do of all lone mothers. In addition, Table 2.3 indicates that lone divorced fathers have represented a faster-growing proportion of all lone fathers over the past fifteen or so years than have divorced lone mothers of all lone mothers.

Table 2.3 also shows the trend in the composition of one-parent families since 1971 according to whether the head of family was a lone mother or father. There has been a steady increase in the proportion of one-parent families headed by a lone mother – from 86 to 91 per cent – and a corresponding decrease in the proportion headed by a lone father – from 14 to 9 per cent.

HOUSEHOLDS CONTAINING FAMILIES WITH DEPENDENT CHILDREN

Up to this point only families with dependent children have been considered, but in order to appreciate the full extent of the demographic changes which have taken place over the last few decades, it is informative to consider how the composition of households has altered over the period. In this way, it may be seen how the relative growth in the number of one-parent families – and relative decline in the number of married couples with dependent children – has affected the relative numbers of other types of family. Table 2.4 brings together historical and

Table 2.4 Families within households (percentages), by type of household, 1961–88, Great Britain

Type of household	Census			General household survey	
	1961	1971	1981	1984	1988
One-family households*					
All lone parents with dependent children	2.3	2.8	4.7	4.4	4.8
Lone parent with 1 dependent child	1.4	1.4	2.4	2.4	2.6
Lone parent with 2 dependent children	0.6	0.8	1.5	1.3	1.4
Lone parent with 3 or more dependent children	0.3	0.6	0.7	0.6	0.8
Lone parent with non-dependent children	4.5	3.9	3.7	3.7	3.6
All married couples with dependent children	38	34	31	29	26
Married couple with 1 dependent child	17	13	12	11	10
Married couple with 2 dependent children	13	13	13	13	11
Married couple with 3 or more dependent children	8	9	6	5	5
Married couple with non-dependent children	10	9	8	8	8
Married couple only	26	27	26	26	28
Two or more family households	2.7	1.4	0.9	0.7	0.7
No family households	17	22	26	28	29
All households	100	100	100	100	100
Equivalent sample size† (thousands)	1620	1830	1950	9.8	10.2

*Dependent children are defined as aged under 16 or 16 to 18 and in full-time education.
†Forms base of 100 per cent; census figures are derived from 10 per cent sample tables.

current data on all types of families within households from the results of several censuses and General Household Surveys.

Between 1961 and 1981, within single-family households, the proportion of families which were classified by the census as lone-parent families doubled from 2.3 to 4.7 per cent; the increase was slightly smaller amongst lone-parent families where there was only one dependent child, but greater than twofold amongst lone-parent families consisting of two or three or more dependent children. In contrast, the corresponding proportions generally fell for married-couple families with dependent children within single-family households. In addition, lone parents with non-dependent children living in single-family households declined slightly as a proportion of all households between 1961 and 1981, as also did the corresponding proportion for married-couple families with non-dependent children. In general, all these trends continued between 1981 and 1988.

Several other related aspects are worth noting from Table 2.4. Multi-family households were only one-third as frequent in 1981 as in 1961, and such multi-family households would have contained additional lone-parent families. Multi-family households formed less than 1 per cent of all households in 1981, and this proportion declined further between 1981 and 1988. The total number of households increased by one-fifth between 1961 and 1981, partly due to a decline in multi-family households and to growth in the overall population, but largely due to a rise in the number of households containing individuals who did not form a family unit; such households were relatively half as numerous again in 1981, compared with 1961. Most of these latter households contained one person living alone; in 1988, 26 per cent of all households were one-person households.

FAMILY SIZE OF ONE-PARENT AND MARRIED-COUPLE FAMILIES

The numbers of dependent children in lone-mother and lone-father families have changed over the years, as Table 2.5 indicates. Since the early 1970s there has been an increase in the relative number of lone-mother families which contain only one or two dependent children and a corresponding decrease in the

Table 2.5 One-parent families and married-couple families (percentages), by number of dependent children,* 1971–88, Great Britain

Type of one-parent family	Year	Number of dependent* children					Sample no. of families†	Type of family	Number of dependent* children					Sample no. of families†
		1	2	3	4 or more	Total			1	2	3	4 or more	Total	
Lone mothers	1971–73	52	29	12	8	100	(1050)	Lone fathers	60	25	10	5	100	(156)
	1975–77	53	30	11	6	100	(1237)		48	33	14	5	100	(174)
	1979–81	55	31	9	5	100	(1380)		55	31	12	1	100	(194)
	1982–84	55	31	10	3	100	(1253)		56	29	13	2	100	(127)
	1986–88	55	30	11	4	100	(1314)		66	28	5	2	100	(130)
Lone parents	1971–73	53	28	11	8	100	(1206)	Married couples	36	39	17	9	100	(12,856)
	1975–77	52	30	11	6	100	(1411)		36	41	16	7	100	(12,246)
	1979–81	55	31	10	4	100	(1574)		38	43	14	5	100	(11,315)
	1982–84	55	31	11	3	100	(1380)		38	43	14	4	100	(9014)
	1986–88	56	30	11	3	100	(1444)		40	43	13	4	100	(8405)

*Dependent children are defined as aged under 16 or from 16 to 18 (inclusive) and in full-time education.
†Forms based on 100 per cent percentages.
Source: General Household Surveys

57485

relative number with three or more. A similar phenomenon – though even more pronounced – has occurred amongst lone-father families, where the proportion of families with either one or two dependent children has increased from 85 to 94 per cent. However, married-couple families with dependent children – from which most lone-parent families are drawn – have also become smaller since 1971, with the proportion with only one or two dependent children increasing and the proportion with three or more decreasing.

Lone-father families tend to be smaller, on average, than lone-mother families. Currently two-thirds of lone-father families contain only one dependent child, whereas only just over half of lone-mother families do so. In contrast, there are relatively more married-couple families with two dependent children than those with only one.

DEPENDENT CHILDREN IN ONE-PARENT AND MARRIED-COUPLE FAMILIES

The left-hand side of Table 2.6 provides estimates of the average family size of the different type of one-parent families, and also of married-couple families, for selected three-year periods between 1971 and 1988. Overall, the average number of dependent children per family declined over the period from 2.0 to 1.8; so did the average family size of one-parent families (which was already at a lower level) – from 1.8 to 1.6. The average number of dependent children in lone-mother families has consistently been higher than that in lone-father families. One-parent families headed by a lone mother who is single are the only type of lone-mother family where the average family size has not declined. Using the average number of dependent children per one-parent family and the best estimate of the number of one-parent families, the number of dependent children in one-parent families in 1986 is estimated to have been just over 1.6 million.

The right-hand half of Table 2.6 gives the percentage of all dependent children who live in the different types of family. Currently, in a group of one hundred dependent children, about twelve live in one-parent families headed by a lone mother,

Table 2.6 Number of dependent children* in one-parent and married-couple families, 1971–88, Great Britain

Type of family with dependent children*	Average number of dependent children* per family				Sample number of families 1986–88	Of all dependent children* living in families, percentages living in given family type:				Sample number of dependent children* 1986–88
	1971–73	1979–81	1982–84	1986–88	1986–88	1971–73	1979–81	1982–84	1986–88	1986–88
Lone mothers										
Single	1.3	1.2	1.3	1.3	(374)	0.7	1.4	1.9	2.8	(504)
Separated	2.0	1.9	1.9	1.8	(273)	2.5	2.8	2.4	2.8	(504)
Divorced	1.9	1.8	1.7	1.8	(568)	1.9	4.1	5.1	5.7	(1016)
Widowed	1.8	1.5	1.5	1.4	(99)	1.6	1.3	1.3	0.8	(139)
Lone mothers	1.8	1.7	1.6	1.6	(1314)	6.7	9.6	10.7	12.2	(2163)
Lone fathers	1.6	1.6	1.6	1.4	(130)	0.9	1.3	1.1	1.0	(184)
Lone parents	1.8	1.7	1.6	1.6	(1444)	7.6	10.9	11.8	13.2	(2347)
Married-couple families†	2.0	1.9	1.9	1.8	(8405)	92.4	89.1	88.2	86.8	(15375)
All families	2.0	1.9	1.8	1.8	(9849)	100.0	100.0	100.0	100.0	(17722)

*Dependent children are defined as aged under 16 or 16 to 18 and in full-time education.
†Includes some cohabiting couples.
Source: General Household Surveys

whereas only one lives with a lone father. Six in every hundred dependent children live with a divorced lone mother; it has recently been estimated (Haskey, 1990) that, were the composite 1988–9 divorce rate to persist unchanged, almost one in every four children would be affected by divorce before reaching the age of sixteen. Overall, over one in eight children currently lives in a one-parent family. Table 2.6 also shows how these percentages have changed since the early 1970s: the proportion of all dependent children who live in one-parent families has increased by about 15 per cent.

AGES OF DEPENDENT CHILDREN WITHIN
ONE-PARENT AND MARRIED-COUPLE FAMILIES

Table 2.7 shows how the distributions of ages of dependent children within the different types of one-parent families have changed since the early 1970s. Of course, the ages of children in one-parent families reflect not only the cumulative effects of the differing rates of formation of one-parent families in previous years, but also the differing fertility rates of women of the same age as the children's mothers in those years – and the different fertility rates for births both inside and outside marriage.

Overall, the ages of the children in the different types of one-parent families vary according to the ages of the lone parents concerned – discussed below – so that dependent children in lone-single-mother families tend, on average, to be the youngest, and those in lone-widowed-mother families the oldest. Six in every ten dependent children in lone-single-mother families are under five, whilst the corresponding proportion for children in lone-widowed-mother families is only one in ten. Children in separated-lone-mother families tend to be a little younger than those in divorced-lone-mother families, but this finding is understandable given that separation precedes divorce, and separated lone mothers are slightly younger on average than divorced lone mothers – as is confirmed below.

Dependent children in lone-father families are older than those in the different types of lone-mother families – 74 per cent of dependent children in lone-father families are ten or over, whereas the corresponding percentages in single-, separated-,

Table 2.7 Distribution of ages of dependent children* (percentages) within one-parent and married-couple families, 1973–88, Great Britain

Type of family with dependent* children	Ages of dependent* children				
	0–4	5–9	10–15	16–18	All ages
Lone mothers					
Single					
1973–75	58	23	17	1	100
1979–81	52	27	21	0	100
1982–84	60	23	16	1	100
1986–88	60	31	7	2	100
Separated					
1973–75	26	32	38	4	100
1979–81	27	32	37	5	100
1982–84	25	30	40	5	100
1986–88	36	30	30	4	100
Lone fathers					
1973–75	9	26	60	5	100
1979–81	3	18	67	13	100
1982–84	7	14	64	15	100
1986–88	7	19	59	15	100

Type of family with dependent* children	Ages of dependent* children				
	0–4	5–9	10–15	16–18	All ages
Lone mothers					
Divorced					
1973–75	14	33	49	4	100
1979–81	11	29	51	8	100
1982–84	13	29	49	9	100
1986–88	16	30	48	6	100
Widowed					
1973–75	4	24	60	11	100
1979–81	4	12	70	15	100
1982–84	9	16	55	21	100
1986–88	10	21	49	20	100
Married couples					
1973–75	28	32	36	4	100
1979–81†	25	28	39	7	100
1982–84	28	26	39	7	100
1986–88	29	29	35	7	100

*Dependent children are defined as aged under 16 or from 16 to 18 (inclusive) and in full-time education.
†Estimated.
Source: General Household Surveys

divorced- and widowed-lone-mother families are 9, 34, 54 and 70 per cent respectively. It is not surprising that the ages of children in lone-father families should most closely resemble those in widowed-lone-mother families, since widowed lone fathers form one-quarter of all lone fathers, three times the proportion that widowed lone mothers form of all lone mothers (see Table 2.3).

In general, amongst each of the different types of lone-mother families, there has been an increase in the proportions of dependent children under five, under ten and from sixteen to eighteen, but a decrease in the proportion in the ten-to-fifteen age group. However, these trends have not been uniform, and in several of the different types of families – including married-couple families – there is evidence of relatively larger numbers of children who were born in the second half of the 1960s, and relatively fewer children who were born in the mid to late 1970s. This finding partially reflects the fact that the annual number of births was highest in the mid 1960s and fell consistently and sharply throughout the following decade.

AGES OF LONE MOTHERS AND LONE FATHERS IN ONE-PARENT FAMILIES

The ages of lone mothers vary considerably according to marital status, as Figure 2.4(a) indicates. As might be expected, a high proportion – half – of single (never-married) lone mothers are under twenty-five; consequently the median age of single lone mothers is twenty-five. In complete contrast is the age distribution for widowed lone mothers, where relatively few are under thirty-five but comparatively many are forty-five or over. Over one-third of widowed lone mothers are fifty or over, and the estimated median age of widowed lone mothers is forty-five. The age distributions of separated and divorced lone mothers are fairly similar; relatively large numbers are in their thirties. However, 16 per cent of separated lone mothers are under twenty-five, whereas comparatively few – 4 per cent – of divorced lone mothers are of similar age. That separated lone mothers generally tend to be slightly younger than divorced lone mothers is apparent from their median ages – thirty-two and thirty-six respectively.

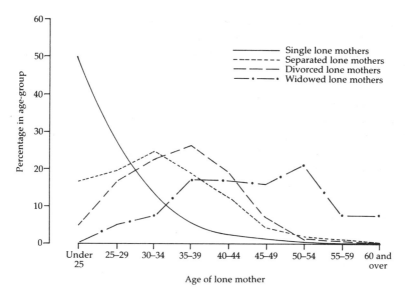

Figure 2.4(a) Ages of lone mothers in one-parent families, by their marital status, 1986–88, Great Britain

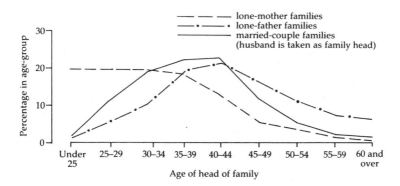

Figure 2.4(b) Ages of heads of families for one-parent and married-couple families with dependent children, 1986–88, Great Britain

Figure 2.4(b) depicts the age distribution of lone fathers, as well as of all lone mothers; in addition, the age distribution of husbands in married-couple families with dependent children is shown. It may be seen that lone fathers tend to be older than fathers in married-couple families, a finding reflected by the fact that their estimated median ages are forty-one and thirty-eight respectively. Only 9 per cent of fathers in married-couple families are fifty or over, whereas the corresponding proportion for lone fathers is 26 per cent. The reason for this lies in the fact that a quarter of lone fathers are widowers – see Table 2.3 – who tend to be older than lone fathers of other marital statuses.

Table 2.8 shows the proportions of lone-parent families who live by themselves, with the lone parent's parents, or with other relatives. In recent years the proportions of separated, divorced and widowed lone mothers living in these different situations have been very similar, with about nine in every ten such lone mothers living alone and a few per cent each living with parents, other relatives or non-relatives. Not surprisingly, a smaller proportion – 73 per cent – of single lone mothers have been living alone, and a greater proportion living with their parents, compared with other lone mothers.

Overall, in more recent years, a higher proportion of lone mothers than of lone fathers have been living alone – 86 and 80 per cent respectively. In addition, about the same proportion of lone mothers as of lone fathers have been living with their parents, or with other relatives, but relatively twice as many lone fathers as of lone mothers have been living in a household in which others, who were not relatives, have been resident.

Table 2.8 also indicates that there has been a growing trend since the early 1970s towards lone-parent families living by themselves – this trend has been particularly pronounced amongst single lone mothers, where the proportion living alone has doubled. Most of this change has occurred through a reduction in the proportion of lone parents who have lived either with their own parents or with other relatives. Again, the change has been greatest for single lone mothers; the proportion living with their own parents in 1986–8, at 16 per cent, was only one-third the corresponding proportion in 1973–5, at 49 per cent. These trends are generally consistent with the reduction in the proportion of households which have contained two or more families; between 1971 and 1988 this proportion halved (see Table 2.4).

Table 2.8 Family circumstances (percentages) of one-parent families, 1973–88, Great Britain

Type of one-parent family with dependent* children	Living alone	With parents	With other relatives	With non-relatives	Total
Lone mothers					
Single					
1973–75	36	49	7	8	100
1979–81	54	37	3	6	100
1982–84	56	31	6	7	100
1986–88	73	16	3	8	100
Separated					
1973–75	78	13	3	6	100
1979–81	80	10	3	7	100
1982–84	86	7	3	4	100
1986–88	92	3	2	3	100
Lone mothers					
1973–75	72	18	4	6	100
1979–81	77	12	3	8	100
1982–84	79	11	4	6	100
1986–88	86	7	2	5	100
Lone mothers					
Divorced					
1973–75	74	15	4	7	100
1979–81	83	6	2	9	100
1982–84	85	6	3	6	100
1986–88	91	4	1	4	100
Widowed					
1973–75	88	7	4	2	100
1979–81	88	4	6	2	100
1982–84	88	3	7	2	100
1986–88	90	2	3	5	100
Lone fathers					
1973–75	70	12	8	10	100
1979–81	82	7	4	7	100
1982–84	78	8	4	10	100
1986–88	80	6	2	12	100

*Dependent children are defined as aged under 16 or from 16 to 18 (inclusive) and in full-time education.
Source: General Household Surveys

LONE PARENTS BY ETHNIC GROUP

There are some pronounced differences in the prevalence of lone-parent families between the different ethnic minority communities (Haskey, 1986). Figure 2.5 shows the composition of households by type of family according to the ethnic group of the head of household. Overall, 11 per cent of households headed by a person from one of the ethnic minority populations consist of a one-family lone-parent household, higher than the corresponding proportion of 4 per cent for households headed by a person from the white population.

There is considerable variation between households headed by members of the different ethnic groups; almost one in four households headed by a West Indian contains a one-parent family living alone, and the corresponding proportion for African households is one in nine, the second-highest proportion. One-parent families are relatively uncommon within one-family households headed by persons from the Chinese, Indian, Pakistani and Bangladeshi ethnic groups – around one in twenty. In contrast, one-family households consisting of a couple with dependent children form a high proportion – approximately two-thirds – of all Indian, Pakistani and Bangladeshi households. Less than one-third of white, West Indian and African households contain such families.

Figure 2.5 also reveals that multi-family households containing children are relatively much more frequent amongst ethnic minority households than white households; the proportions are 5 and 1 per cent respectively. A few additional one-parent families with dependent children would be resident in such multi-family households, although it is doubtful whether they would add more than one or two percentage points to the proportions of households consisting of a single-family lone-parent family.

GEOGRAPHICAL VARIATION IN THE PREVALENCE OF ONE-PARENT FAMILIES WITHIN GREAT BRITAIN

As mentioned earlier, a 'best estimate' of the number of one-parent families in Great Britain has been made in more recent

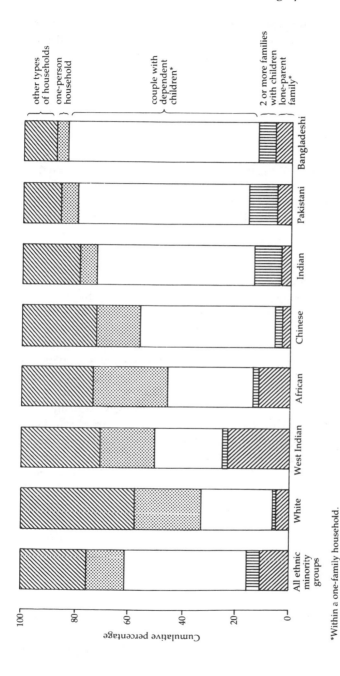

*Within a one-family household.

Source: Labour Force Surveys

Figure 2.5 Percentage of households which contain a lone parent with dependent children,* by ethnic group of head of household, 1986–88, Great Britain

years – by deriving alternative estimates from different sample survey data sources, and using several different estimation methods. These alternative estimates vary, and the value of each has its own associated uncertainty (Haskey, 1989a) as a result of sampling variability. Consequently it is inadvisable, on the grounds of reliability, to try to produce regional or local estimates by the same method, or alternatively to attempt to disaggregate the national 'best estimate' into component regional or local estimates.

However, even though the data and methods which have been used in recent years are not robust enough to produce estimates of sub-national numbers of one-parent families, some information, derived from the 1981 census, can be used to give an impression of the geographical variation in the prevalence of one-parent families. Although the 1981 census did not include the full range of questions needed to provide statistics of one-parent families according to the required definition, one particular variable tabulated in the Census County Reports – see inset to Figure 2.6 for details – is judged to be strongly correlated with the number of one-parent families. By considering the concentration of one-parent families in each area expressed as a percentage of that for Great Britain as a whole – that is, the relative concentration – certain disadvantages of using census data are reduced in their effect. In addition, the relative geographical differences are unlikely to have changed radically since 1981, even though the absolute number of one-parent families in Great Britain has risen since then – by an estimated 19 per cent.

Figure 2.6 depicts the resulting relative concentrations calculated for each county of England and Wales, and for each region (county equivalent) of Scotland. Almost invariably, it is the metropolitan counties which show the highest relative concentrations of one-parent families. However, the comparatively small number of counties with very high relative concentrations (see inset to Figure 2.6) are counterbalanced by a much larger number of counties, mostly rural, where the relative concentration of one-parent families is well below the national average.

Census data are, of course, also available for areas below county level, the Table 2.9 gives the twenty county districts with the highest relative concentrations of one-parent families in Great Britain. London boroughs predominate in this list, as do some of the larger cities (Leicester and Birmingham just miss being

Table 2.9 Proportion (expressed as a percentage of the proportion for Great Britain) of the number of households containing dependent children* which contain at least one one-parent family – areas at county district level within Great Britain with the highest values, 1981

Order	Area	County/Region in which contained	Percentage[†]
1	Lambeth	Greater London	230
2	Hackney	Greater London	223
3	Hammersmith	Greater London	210
4	Islington	Greater London	202
5	Southwark	Greater London	202
6	Camden	Greater London	200
7	Westminster	Greater London	187
8	Kensington and Chelsea	Greater London	185
9	Wandsworth	Greater London	185
10	Tower Hamlets	Greater London	181
11	Manchester	Greater Manchester	178
12	Lewisham	Greater London	170
13	Haringey	Greater London	162
14	Nottingham	Nottinghamshire	160
15	Brent	Greater London	150
16	Glasgow City	Strathclyde Region	145
17	Liverpool	Merseyside	141
18	Brighton	East Sussex	139
19	Greenwich	Greater London	136
20	Dundee City	Tayside Region	134

*Under 25, never married and in full-time education.
[†]Of corresponding proportion for Great Britain (14.1 per cent).
Source: 1981 census

included). It may be seen that East Sussex has a high relative concentration because of that of Brighton. Possibly the formation rate of one-parent families is much higher in urban than in rural areas, or perhaps lone parents move to these areas for economic, social or other reasons.

CONCLUSION

Although this chapter has given estimates of the numbers of one-parent families and described some of their features, the fact remains that statistical information on their social, demographic

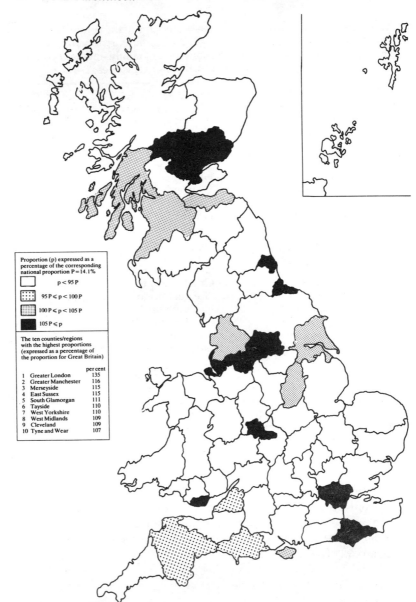

Figure 2.6 Proportion of households containing dependent children*
which contain at least one one-parent family, 1981, Great Britain

*Aged under 25, never married and in full-time education.

The census variable used as a proxy for the number of one-parent families in a given area in 1981 – from which the geographical variations in the concentration of one-parent families have been estimated

The variable used is the 'number of households with dependent children which contain at least one one-parent family'. This variable does not equate with the number of one-parent families because:

a. it involves households as well as families
b. the definition of dependent children differs (it is those aged under 16, or those aged from 16 to [under] 25 and in full-time education)
c. – quite apart from a. and b., the one-parent family identified by the census algorithm does not always coincide with the required definition (see Section 1.2)

The concentration of one-parent families in a given area, A, C_A, has been estimated by:

$$C_A = \frac{\text{number of households with dependent children (in area A) which contained at least one one-parent family}}{\text{total number of households (in Area A) with dependent children}}$$

Then the relative (with respect to the average for Great Britain GB) concentration R_A, for a given area A was defined as:

$$R_A = \frac{C_A}{C_{GB}} \times 100$$

The extent to which R_A is above or below 100 is likely to be highly correlated with the corresponding figure for one-parent families.

and financial characteristics is limited. This is partly because the creation or disappearance of a one-parent family is not always as clear-cut an event as, say, a birth or a death; consequently the appropriate full-scale databases often do not exist. As a result, reliance has to be placed upon the findings from various sample surveys which, by their nature, yield estimates subject to uncertainty. Also, the questions posed in representative sample surveys do not always provide the means of making estimates on alternative definitions – estimates which would throw light on the relative numbers of lone parents in a variety of different circumstances.

One conclusion is inescapable from the available evidence: there is considerable diversity amongst the different types of lone parents, however defined – a subject explored elsewhere (Crow and Hardey, 1991). Thus a lone widower with dependent children is likely to be in a very different position – regarding social circumstances and economic status – from that of a single lone mother. This diversity is well illustrated by the variation in the tendency to live alone/with relatives and in the area/type of housing in which lone parents live (Haskey, 1989a; Crow and Hardey, this volume, pp. 47–65). These variations are perhaps best understood in terms of the processes by which one-parent families are formed. The demographic histories of lone parents also give a good guide to how they cope with their situation and their subsequent social and economic position, subjects which are covered in greater detail in the following chapters of this book.

NOTE

Any error of fact or interpretation contained in this chapter is the responsibility of the author, as is any opinion expressed, which is not necessarily that of OPCS.

3 The housing strategies of lone parents

Graham Crow and Michael Hardey

There is, as Holme has noted, 'evidence that one-parent families do badly in housing' (1985, p. 40). Lone-parent households are far less likely than their two-parent counterparts to be owner-occupiers and far more likely to be tenants or to be homeless. Within the rented sector of the housing market, lone parents are more likely to occupy accommodation of inferior quality. In particular, lone mothers are prominent among those groups of disadvantaged people who 'tend to get very much worse council housing: older rather than newer; flats rather than houses; higher floors rather than lower' (Harrison, 1983, p. 225). Lone parents are also to be found sharing accommodation with relatives and friends, 'living insecure lives involving frequent moves and being at high risk of homelessness' (Pascall, 1986, p. 148). In addition, lone parents are more likely to live in inner-city than suburban locations (Archbishop of Canterbury's Commission, 1985; Haskey, this volume, pp. 40–3). In both a tenurial and a geographical sense, lone-parent households are concentrated in the poorer parts of the urban system.

Housing problems among lone-parent households are by no means unique to the present day. The Finer Report (DHSS, 1974) concluded that housing presented single-parent families with their most serious problem after financial difficulties, reflecting both their low incomes and discrimination in the allocation of local-authority properties. A similar picture of housing disadvantage emerged from Marsden's *Mothers Alone* (1973), George and Wilding's *Motherless Families* (1972) and Cashmore's *Having To* (1985). In turn, these studies are preceded by a long history of lone parents experiencing disadvantage in their housing situation due to their poor market position and their identification as 'less deserving' of assistance than two-parent families (Page, 1984). Typical of this history are the 1950s designation of single mothers as 'unsatisfactory tenants' (Rose, 1985, p. 247) and the more recent classification by a local authority of single-parent families as 'problem tenants' or 'difficult tenants' (Karn and Henderson, 1983, pp. 72–3).

The marginal and stigmatised position of lone-parent house-holds exposes housing policy's failure to respond adequately to their needs. Despite the recurrent anticipation of changes in social policy bringing relief to lone parents, the general con-clusion of researchers is that not enough has been done to avoid the majority of lone-parent households being locked into a disadvantaged position. In recent years this has involved their being caught up, along with other 'atypical households' (Karn and Henderson, 1983), at the wrong end of the process of social polarisation (Townsend *et al.*, 1987). The sale of council houses following the 1980 Housing Act and the curtailment of new housing provision in the public sector have increased social polarisation by leaving the remaining public housing stock dominated by poor households. For lone parents, housing policy has not only failed to counter the process of social polarisation but has actually contributed to it (Forrest and Murie, 1988; Willmott and Murie, 1988). Lone-parent households constitute a signifi-cant element of the most disadvantaged section of society which is increasingly referred to, albeit contentiously, as the 'under-class' (Bulmer, 1989; Field, 1989).

DIVERSITY IN THE HOUSING SITUATIONS OF LONE-PARENT HOUSEHOLDS

Although lone-parent households in general are subject to housing disadvantage relative to two-parent households, it is important to recognise that there is a good deal of diversity within the broad category of 'lone-parent households'; in their experi-ence of housing, some lone-parent households fare noticeably worse than others. Holme is careful to record that young single mothers are particularly likely 'to suffer a stressful history of housing instability' (1985, p. 40), and her study found them typically staying, involuntarily and insecurely, with their parents. Relative to this group, widows and lone fathers occupy a more favourable position, with the fortunes of divorced and separated mothers somewhere in between (Pascall, 1986).

The diversity to be found amongst lone-parent households matters, since the various groups' routes into lone parenthood divide them not only in terms of their current access to housing resources but also in terms of the strategies they can employ for securing and enhancing their position in the future. With varying room for manoeuvre in the housing market, many of the options open to more advantaged lone parents are closed off to the most disadvantaged. The unequal power of lone parents in the housing market means that the impact of the process of social polarisation on lone parents will be uneven rather than uniform, and global figures for the broad category of 'lone parents' will disguise the situation of those closest to the negative pole, for whom choices are the most constrained. The situation of those at the bottom of the pile is aptly described as one of *Having To* (Cashmore, 1985). For others who are able to exercise a greater degree of control over their lives, strategic considerations regarding economic, geographical and cultural aspects of housing and community life will play a larger part in shaping their housing careers. In both cases, the range of choices and constraints is being reshaped by the general process of social polarisation.

Divisions within the broad category of 'lone-parent households' are linked to marked diversity in their housing careers. While some writers estimate that between a quarter and a third of lone parents share accommodation with other adults (Millar, 1987; Pascall, 1986), the proportion is higher for never-married mothers, who 'often move back or continue to live with their own parents in three-generational households' (Leonard and Speakman, 1986, p. 50), and used to be higher still (McDowell, 1983; Walker, 1988; Haskey, this volume, pp. 38–9). Such arrangements can be fraught, especially where they result in overcrowding and a lack of privacy. In the longer term, never-married mothers are increasingly likely to move on from shared accommodation to public-sector housing. Owner-occupation is an unlikely destination, housing only a small and declining fraction of never-married mothers (Haskey, 1989a; Murphy, 1989), while opportunities to rent privately have also shrunk – markedly so among those dependent on state benefits (Forrest and Murie, 1988).

There is less imbalance between the public and owner-occupied sectors in the housing situations of lone parents who are separated or divorced, indicating that a greater proportion of this group commence their parenthood as owner-occupiers. Since people's quality of housing reflects their income, wealth and work status, the socioeconomic situation of lone parents before separation will have a significant influence on their subsequent position in the housing market. Haskey estimates that 'lone mothers as a whole are almost twice as likely as all households headed by women to be in the process of buying their home' (1989a, p. 33), but over the longer term there is a trend towards dependence on the local-authority sector and away from owner-occupation. Lone-parent households are prominent among those officially classified as homeless, and although those which follow this route into local-authority housing are given priority (Willmott and Murie, 1988), they tend to be offered poorer-quality accommodation (Millar, 1987). Homeless lone parents 'are frequently given only one offer of accommodation, which is often in a poor state of repair, on a run-down estate or in a high-rise block' (Watson, 1988, p. 32). The probability of such offers being accepted is a telling indicator of the paucity of alternatives to the local-authority sector and the effectiveness of limiting the number of offers made to a household applying for local-authority housing.

The diversity found among lone parents' housing careers is unsurprising when it is remembered that they number over one million (Haskey, this volume, p. 22). Like other household types, lone-parent households are 'only categorically alike' (Wallman, 1984, p. 109), divided by their routes into and potential routes out of lone parenthood, and by their varying access to resources. Jackson argues that the poorest of all are lone mothers who have several children to bring up, whose lives are likely to mean 'poor housing, sharing bedrooms, basic food, worries over fuel and other bills, no holidays' (1982, p. 174). The options for such lone parents are constrained by their poorer education and earning power, and members of this group are less likely than other lone parents to marry or remarry. As Sullivan concludes, 'marital breakdown exacerbates the housing disadvantage experienced by those who are already disadvantaged in other respects' (1986, p. 48).

At the other extreme are those who pass through lone parenthood only briefly. Ermisch has shown that 'quite a large proportion of lone mothers are in that state for a relatively short period' (1989, p. 52), with half of single mothers and a third of divorced mothers leaving lone parenthood within three years. In addition, not all lone parents are poor (Jackson, 1982), and although researchers have tended not to focus on the better off, it is clear that some groups of lone parents are less vulnerable than others. The strategies which they are able to devise in order to secure their housing objectives play a crucial role in determining how successfully they can resist the downward pressure on lone parents which the process of polarisation in general exerts.

THE HOUSING STRATEGIES OF LONE PARENTS

Two contrasting pictures of lone parenthood can be painted, one emphasising choice and the other constraint. Choice has been detected, for example, over where lone mothers live. In contrast to conventional male-headed households, 'households comprised of single people, and especially single women (with or without children), do not value suburban housing so greatly. For them, access to other single people will be more significant and private renting will often be the preferred form of housing tenure' (Abercrombie *et al.*, 1988, p. 327). Choice also plays some part in Champion's account, reminiscent of the work of the Chicago School, of the housing options facing disadvantaged groups:

. . . the inner city forms the 'sink' to which gravitates a range of marginal and minority groups, including non-white immigrants, young single people, one-parent families and various types of social deviants who prefer the anonymity of big-city life or who have been ostracized by their community of origin (1989, pp. 125–6).

In contrast to approaches which emphasise choice, Cashmore's account attaches little importance to preferences, concentrating instead on the compulsion to which lone parents are subject: 'Oneparenthood . . . is a labyrinth . . . from which there is no escape. . . . Once at the mercy of the local council housing department one's choice of accommodation is disarmingly limited.' Enmeshed in multiple deprivation, such lone parents 'constitute perhaps the most deprived group in modern society: the poorest, the worst-housed, the least-advantaged, caught in a network from which they don't have the resources to break away'

(1985, p. 200). Likewise, Austerberry and Watson include single parents among those 'families who are desperate for housing [and] are forced to accept bad housing offers simply because they have no other choice' (1985, p. 100), while in similar vein Pascall observes that 'those in desperate need accept places that would be turned down by those under less pressure' (1986, p. 135). The same explanation is applied to sharing accommodation: 'it is unrealistic to see it as chosen in most cases and more realistic to see it as homelessness' (1986, p. 148).

Part of the difference between these two views can be accounted for by the use of different types of lone-parent households as examples, but only at the extremes are completely free choice and compulsion to be found. In general, 'access to different types of housing is determined by "constraint" as well as "choice" (Murphy, 1989, p. 101), and for many lone-parent households the situation is best described as one of constrained choice, a situation in which the strategies devised by those involved have a crucial bearing on the outcome.

Given their diversity, there is no one ideal strategy for lone parents to follow, but it is possible to make certain generalisations about the options open to the various types of lone-parent household. In addition, the extent to which lone parents have real choices to make between different housing options can be taken as a measure of how successfully social policies in this area are operating, and how far they are able to counteract the restriction of choice associated with the process of social polarisation. The argument developed below is supported by evidence derived from qualitative research among lone parents living in Birmingham, London and the South-East, carried out by Michael Hardey. The interviews from which the quotations are drawn were conducted in 1988 amongst a sample of lone parents who had been on their own for at least a year and whose names have been changed to preserve anonymity.[1]

Staying put

The majority of lone-parent households are created by separation or divorce, and staying put in the matrimonial home may be considered desirable from the point of view of minimising the disruption to children's lives of parental separation (Eekelaar and Maclean, 1986; Logan, 1986), but it is more likely to be the long-term outcome for those in local-authority housing than it is for either owner-occupiers or those in privately rented accommodation. Among owner-occupiers, only a minority of the lone-parent households in Eekelaar and Maclean's study managed to stay put, and 'the children moved in about three quarters of all owner-occupier cases' (Eekelaar, 1984, p. 92). In Sullivan's (1986) analysis of data from the Family Formation Survey, the change was even more dramatic: the proportion of women living in owner-occupied single-family homes fell from 34 to 7 per cent in the wake of family dissolution.

Of course, not all lone parents will want to stay in the matrimonial home, given its associations with a lost family life, while others may want to move away from the area (Eekelaar and Maclean, 1986), but there are many ties which it is desirable to maintain if at all possible. As Judith explained, referring to her ex-husband:

> I had put up with a lot from him over the years because I did not want to lose my home, but when I found out that I could stay on in it, well I went ahead and started the divorce. Keeping the house on was important to me because it meant that the kids would still have their home, they were settled in at school and I have some good mates on the estate. I don't think I could have managed if there weren't people nearby who would help out when I needed it.

In addition, in straightforward economic terms staying put is probably the best option among owner-occupiers where the financial situation allows (Hart, 1976; Pascall, 1986). Aware that sale of her matrimonial home threatened a financial loss, a former lone parent in Burgoyne and Clark's study who had subsequently remarried saw herself as 'sitting on a . . . goldmine' so long as she stayed put, with 'sitting tight and trying to cope' (1984, p. 139) her best strategy.

In the long term, the strategy of staying put in the matrimonial home may become progressively more difficult to sustain for lone parents who are owner-occupiers, with mortgage arrears forcing people to sell up and move, but the period of time which elapses before this point arrives can be fairly lengthy (Took and Ford,

1987). The process of negotiation between former partners is often complex, and settlements reached remain vulnerable to pressures for renegotiation, as Kate's account indicates:

> Technically we can live here until the children leave home, after which the house has to be sold. My ex resents us staying here and now that he has remarried and is living abroad he can be very awkward when it comes to maintenance and things. He had a big mortgage on the house which I cannot hope to pay off. He's offered me some money if I will let the house go and has made everything connected with the house a great hassle to try and wear me down. I think now that it would be better if I let the place go because it has become a constant worry. I could get a smaller house nearby and I would quite like to set up a new home which would be just mine and the children's.

The actual conditions under which household dissolution takes place can have a formative effect on the later circumstances of lone-parent households. An amicable separation and the ongoing involvement of the former partner with the lone-parent household does, as Clare explained, play a significant part in her housing situation:

> John has been very good. He wanted us to stay in the house even though it is really too big for the three of us. He felt that it was important that the children should keep the home environment that they were used to. The only disadvantage is that as time goes on I remain dependent upon him, and this may be a problem if I ever met someone I wanted to have a close relationship with.

In different ways both cases show the sorts of problems, both material and emotional, which arise for lone mothers from continuing dependence following divorce. Angela responded to her ex-husband's unreliability regarding maintenance by using her home as a resource in order to stay put there and reduce her dependence on him: 'I could see that he was going to cut himself off from us. I didn't want to keep chasing him for money so I took in a lodger from the college to help pay for the house.'

One of the main reasons for the tenacity with which the strategy of staying put in owner-occupied accommodation is pursued is the unattractiveness of the alternatives. The option of 'buying down' – selling the present property and buying a less expensive one – generally involves a loss of space, involvement in repair work, and the disruption to social networks that comes from moving to another area, and in one way or another is likely to be a negative move (Watson, 1988). Certainly this was Maureen's experience of 'buying down':

> Friends who have known me for a long time say that I started at the top and have worked my way down! I didn't want to be dependent on him [her ex-husband] and it was agreed that the house would be sold. I got half the sale and an extra sum which paid for most of this house. I have moved from one of the 'better' neighbourhoods of Birmingham to one of the poor areas. I see it as the price I pay for independence.

Private renting may be more expensive than keeping up the mortgage repayments, and although lone parents with dependent children may be given priority as homeless persons (Murphy, 1989) there is no guarantee that the accommodation which is offered will be adequate to their needs or commensurate with their wishes (Austerberry and Watson, 1985). Nevertheless, the overall picture is that staying put in the matrimonial home is not an easy option for owner-occupiers in that 'divorce and separation tend to lead women towards the local authority sector' (Pascall, 1986, p. 145).

Among lone-parent households created by divorce which had been living in local-authority accommodation before separation, staying put is much more common (Eekelaar, 1984). The transfer of a tenancy is less complex than the legal processes surrounding the division of the owner-occupied family home, and there is an established system of income support relating to housing which can be mobilised early in the process of household dissolution. Of course, staying put is not a particularly attractive strategy for those whose matrimonial home is poor-quality accommodation, and here it is relevant to note that local-authority housing, like shared housing, is associated with higher-than-average rates of marital dissolution (Murphy, 1989; Thornes and Collard, 1979). And if the strategy of staying put in the matrimonial home following divorce is not universally desirable among those for whom it is possible, for other lone parents it is not even a possibility.

Seeking more appropriate accommodation

There are many reasons for the fact that staying put may not secure appropriate accommodation for lone-parent households, most obviously financial considerations where the housing becomes too expensive to keep up with following the departure of one parent, and inappropriateness of the housing to begin with. Since opportunities for lone parents to enter owner-occupation and private renting are restricted, the destination for the great majority of those lone parents who do not stay put is rented accommodation in the public sector. The adequacy of the accommodation allocated to lone parents by local authorities has, however, frequently been brought into question. Lone-parent households are at the wrong end of the polarisation process in two senses, according to the type of accommodation and the area: 'these families tend to be placed in the worst housing or on the worst estates' (Austerberry and Watson, 1985, p. 100). Nevertheless, the local-authority sector remains the best hope for substantial numbers of lone-parent households, and currently houses 44 per cent of lone fathers and 59 per cent of lone mothers, including 80 per cent of mothers who have never been married (Haskey, 1989a).

Included among those lone-parent households approaching local authorities as homeless will be many to whom any local-authority housing will be an improvement on their existing situation. They may well find themselves offered hard-to-let property, since people with fewer options are more likely to accept such offers. In addition, there is a whole set of beliefs about lone parents as a constituent group of the 'undeserving poor', for whom conventional family housing is not particularly suitable. Two long-standing ideas influencing the allocation of properties are that it is acceptable for lone parents to share a bedroom with a child, and that lone parents are better suited to flats because they are unable to look after houses with gardens (Austerberry and Watson, 1985; Karn and Henderson, 1983).

As a consequence of being identified as less 'respectable' than conventional families, lone parents were among those 'atypical households' which Karn and Henderson found to be receiving 'unfavourable treatment either in being less likely to be accepted for council housing at all or in receiving a disproportionate amount of the worst property on the worst estates' (1983, p. 71). Among ethnic minorities the unfavourable treatment of lone-parent households was even more marked, supporting the view that there is a relationship between preparedness to accept hard-to-let property and paucity of alternatives. Many individuals have little choice but to move during the course of becoming a lone parent. Ann lived alone as a private tenant and was compelled to move when her pregnancy was revealed:

> I had this nice little place but someone must have told the landlord I was expecting. I got these letters and then some visits from the landlord who told me that I had to leave because children were not allowed in the block. I was a good tenant but it was made very clear to me that I would have to go.

A second group of lone-parent households for whom staying put is not a viable option are the victims of domestic violence who need to leave and stay away from the matrimonial home to avoid the danger of assault to themselves or their children. In Pahl's (1985) small-scale study of battered wives who left their home for the safety of a refuge, returning on a long-term basis was a far less likely outcome than eventually setting up home elsewhere.

A third group of lone parents who are forced to move are those whose sharing arrangements with relatives break down. Eleanor began her married life with her husband's parents, but when he left her and their baby it proved impossible to stay:

> I camped out at a friend's flat for a couple of weeks. Luckily we had been on the housing list since we were married, so I got this council place quite quickly. It's not what I would have chosen, but I just had to have somewhere to live. I hope I don't sound ungrateful but I think it's unfair that you can't move to a better place once you move into a flat. The council said I could try for an exchange but that's a joke because no one would want to come to this estate with its reputation.

Hard-to-let properties prove hard to leave for tenants who take them on, reinforcing a sense of being trapped.

Chequered housing histories are not uncommon among lone parents. The search for more appropriate accommodation frequently involves several 'temporary' solutions, many of which turn out to last far longer than originally envisaged. Growing pressure on limited public housing stocks has led to a dramatic rise in the number of families in bed-and-breakfast accommodation, where lone-parent households are spending increasing periods of time. Perceived by lone parents as the 'bottom of the pile', life in such hotels is highly restrictive; often rules preclude having visitors on the premises. Joan described herself as a 'permanent guest' in an hotel given over to social security claimants:

> There are five cookers in the basement that are used by thirty families in the hotel. You can imagine the state they get in. There is a queue to use them and then I have to carry hot pots of food three floors up to my room with Tracy with me. We eat out at the chippy which is easier and gets me out of the hotel. I've been here nearly two years. It's depressing because there is no way out until I get rehoused.

Although the problems of sharing accommodation with relatives or friends are widely recognised, it remains an important housing option for lone parents, particularly in the short term. Among the young single mothers in Holme's study, the majority continued to live with, or returned to, their parents' home. Typical of these mothers was the Bethnal Green resident who stated: 'I had no choice but to stay with my mum, because I went to the council with my boyfriend and they said they didn't have anywhere for me to stay' (1985, p. 41). However, Holme's observation of financial and affective support from parents for the young mothers and their babies is at odds with Cashmore's (1985) findings, which place more emphasis on the friction inherent in such situations and the pressures, both subtle and direct, to leave.

The potential of kinship networks to play a supportive role is illustrated by the following account of how grandparents provided a home for a young mother of twenty and her two-year-old son:

> We'd be in bed and breakfast if it wasn't for me nan. Me mum and dad were very upset when I fell for Craig but me nan has been great and put us up. It isn't ideal and I want to get my own place but there are no council places any more. I mean I can't have friends round and I have to fit in with how me nan likes to keep the house. We get on each other's nerves sometimes and I'd like to have more privacy, but she is very good with Craig.

Shared accommodation can also provide a route into owner-occupation with the combination of separate incomes. Mary and Sandra had known each other for many years, and both worked as teachers in a local school. As Mary noted:

> I lived in a flat and wanted a garden for Jenny [her daughter] and I knew that Sandra was unhappy, because her landlord wouldn't do any repairs. So we decided to try and get a house between us. We both have jobs but teachers are not well-paid and I think building societies thought it a bit odd for two women to set up home together. I used to say that one of us should have a sex change! Anyway, we found this house and got the money for it. It's been fine. We're both better off and our kids get on most of the time.

Obviously there will be great variation in the way sharing with relatives or friends works out. It is at once less isolated and less private than living as a lone parent, allowing access to better domestic facilities but not qualifying as 'a home of one's own'. While sharing accommodation is often entered into as a short-term measure, it may work against the achievement of longer-term solutions. This is especially so where short stays involve frequent moves, making the retention of employment difficult and preventing the accumulation of points through residence in any one area to qualify for local-authority housing (Watson, 1987). Longer-term sharing arrangements such as the joint payment of a mortgage are by no means easy to set up, but may nevertheless offer the most satisfactory solution available. However, they may also pose problems for the future, such as the potential conflict noted by Mary, who shared with Sandra: 'I don't know what would happen if one of us found a man that she wanted to share the house with'.

The private rented sector of the housing market continues to shrink, and the remaining stock of furnished and unfurnished accommodation appears largely closed to lone parents on low incomes and without savings to act as a deposit. Those lone parents who obtain private rented housing are mindful of their powerlessness. Sue is a black twenty-three-year-old who lives with her young child in two furnished rooms in a 1930s house which has been converted into four flats:

> We live in this dump because I could find nothing else. It's very difficult to find places to rent with children. Most landlords just

don't want to know, and those that do charge more for places they
couldn't let to other people. They take advantage because they
know that you couldn't find another place. So I'm in no position to
stick up for myself and complain about the damp and the smell from
the drain.

Lone parents frequently encountered discrimination in their
search for private-sector housing, many taking it as given than
landlords would not consider offering tenancies to lone mothers
reliant on social security.

In recent years housing associations have grown, encouraged
by the state as an alternative to local-authority housing. Some
established small-scale associations aim to provide housing for
low-income families and can be an important source of accommodation for lone-parent households. Sheila's experience points
to housing associations' potential to provide accommodation
better adapted than conventional housing to the requirements of
lone-parent households. When the lease on her former flat ran
out:

The council put me on the list but I was told that there was no hope
of anything for years. I knew that I could have bed and breakfast but
that seemed like sinking to the bottom. There are two housing
associations in the area and one of them had just got some money
from a charity to refurbish this block for families. We came here
three years ago and it was wonderful. . . . It's really ideal because
the flat is completely private but there is a common lounge
downstairs where residents can arrange things. We have a committee that puts on events and decides things that need doing in the
block. There are other single parents here and we can all support
each other.

Housing associations, 'with their ability to serve the needs of
people in special categories, are a real alternative' (Pascall, 1986,
p.157), but they remain very much a minority tenure type for lone
parents, housing only 4 per cent of lone mothers and 2 per cent of
lone fathers (Haskey, 1989a). In terms of scale, the
housing-association sector is dwarfed by the local-authority
sector, which remains the most likely destination for lone-parent
households seeking different accommodation.

Council housing continues to be the best hope for lone parents
in short-term or other unsatisfactory accommodation seeking to
improve their home conditions. For Joan, who lives in a bed-and-

breakfast hotel, being allocated council accommodation is something she dreams about: 'I have this image of my own little place
in a nice area with a bit of garden where we can become a proper
family at last.' Joan's 'dream' is reality for some lone parents – like
Pamela, who had moved with her children to a council property
in a town outside London:

> When I moved here four years ago the house was brand new. It's
> the nicest place I have ever lived in. It's got central heating, plenty
> of space and a garden. The neighbourhood is pleasant and I can be
> sure that Dennis and Beverly will be safe until I get back from work.
> It's just so much better than where we were before in London.
> There I could not get a job and it was not a very pleasant
> neighbourhood. Our lives have very much changed for the better
> since we have been here.

Such opportunities for people's 'ideal home' to become reality
have decreased with the decline of public housing provision.
With growing pressure on scarce resources in inner-city areas,
lone parents in some localities find themselves concentrated on
so-called 'problem' estates which are not only socially marginal
but also physically decaying. Alison felt herself placed in a
position where she had to fight for what she regarded as
adequate and safe housing within the public sector. She had lived
for three years in a flat on a London estate characterised by social
services as one with 'multiple problem families', where several
properties had become physically unsafe and been boarded up:

> I've had a long struggle with the council. I've got doctors' letters
> which say that the flat was bad for the health of both myself and
> Louise. The council kept sending people round who would agree
> that the damp and things were awful but nothing happened about
> it. I said to my councillor and my MP about it and I've threatened to
> stay in the housing office until something is done. . . . I was in the
> local paper and there was a great fuss . . . they have now told me
> that I will be offered a house in the place I want to go.

Alison's story illustrates the need to 'stick up for yourself'
perceived by many lone parents who want to gain resources for
their family but who experience the procedures of the local
authority as an 'obstacle race' (Pascall, 1986, p. 157). Against this
background, to establish a home as a lone parent can provide a

significant sense of autonomy and personal achievement (Hardey, 1989).

Apart from the actual type and condition of the housing, the area in which it is situated can have a formative impact on life chances. Neighbourhoods with high unemployment and no daycare facilities restrict opportunities for lone parents to supplement their social security income or to enter full-time work. Sybille had worked as a nurse until she separated from her husband and eventually moved to an estate in London, where she described herself as 'trapped':

> I don't like my kids spending time on the streets. I could go back to nursing, but what would I do with the kids? Ideally I would like to move to a better area where I would feel it would be all right to trust someone with the kids if I was working.

As noted above, black lone parents are often subject to racial discrimination in addition to the stigma of lone parenthood, and this can be a further factor producing concentrations of disadvantaged groups in particular areas and tenures (Forrest *et al.*, 1990; Sarre *et al.*, 1989: Williams, 1989). Michelle observed:

> I don't think it's just chance that there are so many black families in this block, the council puts us here. Lots of them are lone parents too. I don't think it's good to put us all together like this because the block gets a bad reputation and just because we are alone with our kids doesn't mean we all get on. But I do have some good mates round here.

Council housing can liberate some lone parents to create a stable and secure home environment, but locks others into a situation where home-making is a constant struggle against a hostile environment and dependence on the state an inevitability.

STRATEGIES, CHOICES AND CONSTRAINTS

Several points arise out of the consideration of lone parents' housing strategies. Strategic analysis can be as revealing about constraints as it is about choices (Crow, 1989), and the constraints on lone parents' housing options are particularly prominent. Given the lack of options open to poor lone parents, individual preferences have, at best, limited significance. In addition, where choices do exist it is not always easy to specify which is the most rational course of action to follow, since lone parents need their housing to be not only habitable but also affordable, safe, and close to work opportunities, social facilities and informal networks of support. Rarely do all these coincide, but identifying their order of priority is difficult. Further, it is clear that strategies evolve over time, not only as requirements change as children grow up but also as a result of negotiations with former partners or housing officials, and as short-term options (such as staying with friends) are exhausted. Lone parents' housing strategies reflect highly constrained choices.

The claim that young women in disadvantaged situations deliberately become mothers in order to improve their housing prospects (Murphy, 1989) greatly oversimplifies the complex interplay of choice and constraint. Holme is prepared to consider the possibility that young women may use motherhood as 'a passport to a home of their own' (1985, p. 42), although she suggests that it may be an unconscious rather than a conscious response to the pressures of inner-city life. In addition she notes that young mothers have the prospect of graduating to local-authority housing only after quite lengthy spells of sharing accommodation with their parents. Even where accommodation is secured, young single mothers become locked into poverty unless they can find work (McRobbie, 1989). The strategy of becoming pregnant in order to secure housing is by no means guaranteed to succeed; securing accommodation is a lengthy, risky process requiring both dedication and luck.

In any event, the great majority of lone parents do not enter into their situation by choice. Once in the situation of being a lone parent, housing and other options frequently turn out to be more restricted than anticipated, and neither the strategy of staying put nor that of seeking more appropriate accommodation is guaranteed to produce a solution to difficulties. Here a further possible strategy needs to be mentioned – that of leaving lone parenthood. Getting married or remarried offers a route out of the housing difficulties of being a lone parent (Burgoyne and Clark, 1984), and the fact that the majority of lone parents leave lone parenthood by this route is a telling indicator of the constraints within which they operate. Others leave lone parenthood by waiting for their children to become adults and leave home, allowing them to begin their lives afresh, like Cashmore's respondent who said: 'I'll still be only 32 when the kid's grown up' (1985, p. 21). Individuals leaving lone parenthood by this latter route do not necessarily find that their housing situation improves, and may well find the reverse; many single women are more disadvantaged in the housing market than single mothers (Pascall, 1986).

Polarisation's two distinct but overlapping senses, geographical and tenurial, leave lone parents disproportionately represented in poorer areas of cities and in rented rather than owner-occupied housing. It is not new for lone-parent households to make up a significant proportion of the population in deprived neighbourhoods (Donnison and Ungerson, 1982), but Byrne's recent report on North Tyneside shows that polarisation is an active process, deepening the trend towards greater spatial inequality. Here, the crucial distinction 'is between households with more than one wage-earner and those which are benefit-dependent' (1989, p. 114). Similarly, it is unsurprising to learn that all but one of the single mothers in Holme's (1985) study of Woodford and Bethnal Green are in the latter (inner-city) area.

As the process of social polarisation proceeds, lone parents' situation at the bottom of the housing market is reinforced. The right to buy local-authority property is merely academic for those single parents 'occupying the worst council housing which neither they nor anyone else would want to buy' (Williams, 1989, p. 172). The decline of local-authority stock arising out of the sale of better housing in turn creates what have variously been called 'sink', 'residual', 'ghetto' or 'dump' estates (Austerberry and Watson, 1985; Harrison, 1983), the 'intensified segregation of the poorest' (Karn and Henderson, 1983, p. 84) and a vicious circle of decline (Champion, 1989). Where such estates are in inner-city or outer locations with few job opportunities, labour-market trends look set to reinforce lone parents' difficulties.

Lone parents' housing difficulties are closely linked to their low incomes and to discrimination in the allocation of properties (Sarre *et al.*, 1989; Watson, 1987). There is little evidence to support the stereotype of lone parents as locked into dependency culture, and plenty to challenge it; lone parents are resourceful and active individuals, as indeed they need to be. The single mothers in Tivers's (1985) study wanted to work, suggesting that assistance in the provision of labour-market openings (or the ability to take them up) is crucial for lifting lone parents out of poverty, just as it is their superior labour-market position which is the principal explanation of lone fathers' less disadvantaged situation. From this point of view, housing's location in relation to employment opportunities or daycare facilities may be the most important feature for lone parents to consider.

The current thrust of social policy is towards 'targeting', and this raises particular difficulties in considering lone-parent households, given their diversity. Lone-parent households are not always easy to identify (Crow and Hardey, 1991) and may suffer from disguised homelessness, but even where they can be efficiently targeted the problem remains that being a lone parent may be only one of several disadvantages, not all of which are escaped through leaving lone parenthood. These, however, are finer points relating to the exercise of targeting which, in housing as elsewhere, has a poor track record. Council house sales were, after all, represented by the Secretary of State for the Environment in 1981 as a measure designed 'to reverse the polarization of society between home owners and council tenants' (quoted in George and Wilding, 1984, p. 191). From experience of this policy to date, it would appear that the key to countering polarisation in housing for lone parents and for other disadvantaged groups lies elsewhere.

NOTE

1. The data on which this chapter is based were collected as part of research for the Alvey DHSS Demonstrator project, funded by the Science and Engineering Council and the Department of Trade and Industry.

4 Patterns of health and illness amongst lone-parent families*

Jennie Popay and Gill Jones

In 1969, in the course of a review of social security provision in Britain, a Committee of Inquiry was established to consider 'the problems of one parent families in our society'. The Finer Committee, which reported in 1974 (DHSS, 1974), concentrated on economic circumstances but also examined other issues, including the welfare implications for children. Since then, though there has been some research on the circumstances of one-parent families (Burnell and Wadsworth, 1981; Essen, 1978; Ferri, 1976; Lambert and Streather, 1980; Millar, 1989; Richards and Dyson, 1982), there has been no systematic study of the implications of lone parenthood for the health and welfare of the adults involved.

There are many reasons why there should be such a study. First, there are a lot of one-parent families in Britain; if lone parenthood does have adverse consequences for health, then a large, and changing, group of men and women are at risk. Second, if we could compare and understand differences in patterns of health between lone parents and parents in couples, we might go a long way towards explaining gender differences in health. Finally, research into the health of lone parents is policy relevant: the amount of social security provision needed for one-parent families is currently causing concern, and there is a move to encourage lone parents into the labour market. These deliberations should take account of the probable effects on the health of lone parents of combining the breadwinner and nurturer roles.

* This chapter is an amended version of a longer paper which was originally published in the *Journal of Social Policy*, vol. 19, no. 4, pp. 499–534. It is reprinted here with kind permission of the publishers, Cambridge University Press.

This chapter is about the health of lone parents, male and female. It is a study of lone parents' experience of health and illness in relation to the material and social context of their lives. We examine the health of lone parents in relation to that of parents in couples, and compare the health of lone mothers with that of lone fathers. We look first at explanatory factors such as marital history and age; we begin to examine the effects on health of combining the breadwinner and nurturer roles; we consider the ways in which successful combination of these roles may depend on the context of lone parenthood, including the socioeconomic circumstances and the availability of outside help with daycare. We offer some explanations of the variation we found in our research, but more research is clearly needed.

PREVIOUS RESEARCH

Existing evidence on the health of lone parents suggests that there may be three important dimensions to their experience of health and illness. First, on a number of indicators, lone mothers and fathers appear to experience worse health than parents in couples. Second, among parents there appear to be gender differences in the type, rates and severity of ill health. Third, there appears to be variation among lone parents which may result from their route into lone parenthood.

The latter is reflected in the relationship between health, gender and current marital status, revealed in analysis of census data. Overall, the married have lower mortality rates than the non-married (single or ex-married), and men have higher mortality rates than women. Among non-married men, lowest mortality is amongst the widowed, followed by the single and then the divorced; among women, lowest mortality is amongst the single, followed by the widowed, with the divorced again having the highest mortality (Fox and Goldblatt, 1982). This analysis did not consider responsibility for children, but does suggest that mortality rates may be higher for lone parents than for parents in couples, particularly if they are divorced or male. There is not necessarily, however, any correspondence between risk of premature death and experience of health and illness. Indeed, a major issue facing health researchers is to explain the consistent finding that while men experience higher mortality rates, women report more ill health (for a discussion, see Verbrugge, 1989). Studies do, however, suggest that lone mothers are in poorer health than married mothers, though the findings of different studies are not always consistent – this is a familiar problem in health research, when different outcome measures are used.

The Finer Committee found a low rate of 'mental disorders' reported by never-married mothers, but no other consistent differences in the experience of marital groups (Hunt *et al.*, 1973). A number of studies have found a higher rate of 'psychological distress' among lone mothers in general compared to married mothers (Blaxter, 1990; Burnell and Wadsworth, 1981; Cox *et al.*, 1987; Graham, 1984; Hunt *et al.*, 1973). However, when age and socioeconomic status were controlled for (Bolden, 1980), the number of GP consultations for psychiatric complaints was found to be identical for lone mothers and married ones, but the rate of consultations for respiratory illness was twice as high among lone mothers.

The few studies that have considered the health of fathers according to their marital status suggest that on some measures (psychological distress, minor physical symptoms, days of restricted activity due to illness, and perceptions about their overall state of health) married fathers report the lowest rate of ill health of all parents. Gender differences among lone parents are also highlighted here, however, since lone fathers appear to have been in better health than lone mothers and of similar health status to married mothers, according to their reports (Clark *et al.*, 1987; Evason, 1980; Hunt *et al.*, 1973).

Research by Reissman and Gerstel (1985) suggests that health problems may vary according to the stage of marital dissolution and the severity of problems associated with it – all of this varying by gender. Men have been found to experience more severe health problems than women around the time of marital breakdown, and divorced men to have more health problems than separated men. Among women, the divorced were found to have fewer problems than the separated.

The importance of the socioeconomic context in which parents live was shown in Bolden's (1980) research referred to above. Other studies have reported similar rates of ill health, both physical and psychological, among lone mothers and married women living in poorer circumstances. Beatson-Hird *et al.* (1989) have recently highlighted the importance of employment status, housing tenure and age of youngest child in determining the health of lone parents. The material circumstances in which women perform their nurturing role may be at least as crucial to their health as their marital status. Overall, the research begins to suggest that it may be their poorer socioeconomic status, rather than their lone-parent status *per se*, which is the chief determinant of health and illness among lone mothers.

There are a number of possible explanations as to why lone parents should have a greater risk of poor health than parents in couples. Many lone parents have experienced the stresses of widowhood or marital breakdown. They are among the poorest groups in our society. The lack of a partner in parenting and breadwinning can create additional physical and emotional demands. All these things – their life history, their relative poverty and the demands of their caring roles – might adversely affect their health, and differences along these dimensions amongst lone mothers and fathers may contribute to the gender differences in the experience of poor health.

THE DATASET

The research reported here formed part of an Economic and Social Research Council-funded study of health and health care in households with dependent children which involved secondary analysis of the General Household Survey (GHS). This is a continuous survey with an annual response of around 30,000 individuals in households in Great Britain (OPCS, 1980, 1981, 1982). In order to study male and female lone parents in sufficient depth, it was necessary to create a subset of the data for lone parents in three consecutive years of the GHS: 1980, 1981 and 1982. Though numbers of lone fathers are still small, we include them in the analysis on the grounds that some data on this somewhat neglected group are better than none.

Lone parents have been defined as adults living with their 'dependent' children (aged under eighteen) in a family unit which does not contain a spouse or partner. The subset therefore contains some parents who say they are living as married, but whose partner is not a household member. The spouse may be living away from home for work purposes or living in an institution; in such cases the parent living in the family is treated as a *de facto* lone parent.

Secondary analysis of the GHS has limitations. For example, some important dimensions of lone-parent status, such as its history or duration, are not recorded. An individual's health status at any one time will be an outcome of both past experience and current circumstances; cross-sectional datasets such as the GHS do not readily allow us to locate the present in a longitudinal framework, though variables such as age, marital status and household position do give some indication of the process of the individual life course. Our analysis is thus a modest attempt to study the experience of health and illness amongst lone parents within a broader social context.

LONE PARENTS' EXPERIENCE OF HEALTH AND ILLNESS

In the course of research on the health of parents (Popay and Jones, 1988) we were struck, as others have been, by the relatively poor 'health status' of lone parents, compared with parents in couples. Table 4.1 shows the contrast in health status on three measures of illness and health: long-standing illness, whether limiting or not; recent illness which has restricted activity in the last two weeks (RRI), and perceptions of health in general over the last year. The latter measure involved three possible responses: good, fairly good, and not good ('poor' in the following text). We have confined our analysis to the first and third of these, rather than combining categories. All three measures are based on reports by the respondents themselves.

It is clear from this table that lone parents report poorer health than parents in couples: they are more likely to have a long-standing illness, including one which limits their activity; they are more likely to have RRI; and they are more likely than parents living in couples to consider their general health over the last twelve months to have been poor.

Apart from the disparities between parents in couples and lone parents, there are, however, sex differences. The table shows that among lone parents, lone fathers report slightly more

Table 4.1 Health status of parents by sex and marital status

Sex Marital status	Men				Women			
	Couples		Lone		Couples		Lone	
	%	base	%	base	%	base	%	base
With long-standing illness	26	(3406)	35	(150)	23	(3453)	31	(1008)
With limiting long-standing illness	14	(3406)	20	(150)	12	(3453)	19	(1008)
With recent restricting illness	9	(3401)	11	(150)	11	(3457)	17	(1092)
Reporting good health in last 12 months	75	(3154)	57	(149)	68	(3411)	54	(1089)
Reporting poor health in last 12 months	6	(3154)	11	(149)	8	(3411)	16	(1089)

Source: GHS, 1981 for couples; GHS, 1980–82 for lone parents

long-standing illness, while lone mothers report more recent restricting illness and are more likely to perceive their health status as poor. Similar differences occur amongst parents in couples. These general gender differences in health and illness may be an outcome of normative gender roles in the home and the labour market, as we have suggested elsewhere (Popay and Jones, 1988).

INDIVIDUAL LIFE HISTORY

The characteristics of the lone-parent population have changed over time. The Finer Committee reported (DHSS, 1974) that for some decades widowhood had been declining as a route to lone parenthood, to be replaced by marital breakdown. There has been further change, and a far greater proportion of lone parents are now divorced rather than separated. There has also been an increase in the proportion of never-married lone mothers. Though some of these have previously been cohabiting, there has been an increase in the number of children living from birth with their never-married mother alone (Haskey, 1986; Kiernan and Wicks, 1990).

In terms of their life histories, lone mothers and lone fathers are thus neither homogeneous nor necessarily equivalent groups. Marital status and age differences by gender are shown in Table 4.2. Only about 12 per cent of the lone parents identified in the GHS were male, and they tended to be older than lone mothers (only 14 per cent of lone fathers were under thirty-five, compared with 48 per cent of lone mothers). Lone fathers also had a different marital history, very few being single. Lone fathers were more likely than lone mothers to be widowed (25 per cent compared with 16 per cent of mothers) or separated (30 per cent compared with 21 per cent). Proportions of divorced were similar. The table shows clearly the relationship between age and marital status: younger parents were more likely to be single, while older parents were more likely to be widowed.

To what extent are these differences in age and marital status associated with differences in health status amongst lone mothers and fathers? Table 4.3 controls for age by restricting the analysis to those over thirty-five. Single lone parents are omitted from the table because numbers of single lone fathers are so small, but it should be noted that single lone mothers are marginally in better health than ex-married lone mothers, probably mainly because they are younger.

Overall it appears that mothers and fathers over thirty-five are equally likely to have a long-standing illness (35 per cent compared with 37 per cent), but lone fathers are less likely to report a recent illness (13 per cent compared with 20 per cent) and are more likely to report their health as good (55 per cent compared with 49 per cent). When these findings are compared with the data in Table 4.1, the effect of age can be seen, since lone parents over thirty-five are in poorer health on these measures than lone parents as a whole.

There is, however, considerable variation across marital status groups, and marital status is related to health differentially according to sex. Amongst women, recent restricting illness and perceptions of general health as poor are most strongly associated with separation. Long-standing illness is most common amongst divorced women. Amongst lone fathers, those who have been widowed report the poorest health: 46 per cent have a long-standing illness, 17 per cent have had a recent restricting illness and only 47 per cent report good health. On each count,

Table 4.2 Marital status of lone parents by age group and sex amongst householders (in percentages)

Sex	Male			Female		
Age	<35	35+	All	<35	35+	All
Married*	5	3	3	9	8	8
Single	10	1	2	24	7	15
Widowed	0	29	25	3	26	16
Divorced	52	38	40	40	41	41
Separated	33	30	30	24	18	21
All (=100%)	(21)	(125)	(146)	(496)	(589)	(1085)

*The table includes parents who say they are married but whose partners do not live in the household.
Source: GHS, 1980–82

Table 4.3 Health status of parents by marital status and sex, controlling for age, amongst lone parents 35 years or over

	Separated		Divorced		Widowed		All*	
	%	base	%	base	%	base	%	base
Lone fathers								
with long-standing illness	43	(37)	24	(46)	46	(35)	37	(123)
with recent restricting illness	8	(37)	13	(46)	17	(35)	13	(123)
reporting good health in last 12 months	51	(37)	67	(46)	47	(34)	55	(122)
reporting poor health in last 12 months	13	(37)	4	(46)	15	(34)	12	(122)
Lone mothers								
with long-standing illness	34	(105)	39	(243)	32	(154)	35	(588)
with recent restricting illness	25	(105)	22	(243)	15	(154)	20	(588)
reporting good health in last 12 months	46	(104)	50	(241)	50	(153)	49	(583)
reporting poor health in last 12 months	25	(104)	17	(241)	14	(153)	18	(583)

*Includes single parents and those married whose partners live outside the household.
Source: GHS

widowers have poorer health than other ex-married men. The overall pattern for lone mothers and fathers is also reversed amongst widows and widowers, with the latter reporting worse health than widows on all counts.

Why should marital status (particularly widowerhood among men and separation among women) affect health in these ways? It could be argued that the process of marital dissolution or widowhood, and resulting lone parenthood, though leading to ill health among both men and women, is experienced differently by them. Widowhood may cause a sudden and more dramatic shift in social roles for men than for women, and perhaps more so than marital breakdown. Already possibly the main bread-winners, men suddenly become responsible for home-making and daycare; women probably combine these roles already. Age may also be a factor here: widowers tend to be older than widows. On the other hand, there is also evidence (Popay *et al.*, 1983) that in material terms (finance, housing, etc.) separation is more disrup-tive for women than for men.

As far as within-gender differences are concerned, widows are less likely than divorced or separated women to have experi-enced a deterioration in their material living standards or a housing move. The poor health of separated women may reflect the social, emotional and material turmoil following on marital breakdown, which stabilises to some extent by the time of divorce (Popay *et al.*, 1983). Whatever the explanations, it appears from our data that marital status is closely linked to lone parents' experience of ill health, and that differences in marital status may explain part of the differences in the health and illness experience of lone mothers and fathers.

SOCIOECONOMIC CIRCUMSTANCES AND HEALTH AND ILLNESS

Despite the heterogeneity noted above, the majority of one-parent families – at least, those headed by a woman – share poor socioeconomic circumstances (Burnell and Wadsworth, 1982; Evason, 1980; Ferri, 1976; Glendinning and Millar, 1987; Millar, 1987; Popay *et al.*, 1983). To what extent, then, might the circumstances in which they live contribute to differences in the experience of ill health amongst lone parents compared with parents in couples, and between lone mothers and fathers? We consider this question in two parts, looking first at material living standards and then at social support and employment status.

Material living standards

Indicators of the material living standards of lone parents available in the GHS include the occupational class of their current or last job, their housing tenure, and their income. Given the disparity in employment status amongst women and men, occupational class cannot equally reflect the life chances of lone mothers and lone fathers. We use housing tenure rather than occupational class, since it allows comparisons between the sexes and is a more suitable indicator of material living standards for parents who are not in current employment. However, housing tenure alone is unlikely to be sensitive to the very different living standards of parents in couple households and lone parents. We have therefore also taken some account of household income.

The income measure we have used is based on whether any individual within a single-family-unit household was in receipt of either of the two means-tested benefits payable at that time – Supplementary Benefit and Family Income Supplement. We assume that if any individual is in receipt of either benefit, their household is living on incomes equal to or below 140 per cent of Supplementary Benefit level. All other households are assumed to have incomes above this level. In Table 4.4 we have applied this measure to those living in council housing, giving us three 'standard of living' groups – home owners, council tenants not in receipt of means-tested benefits, and council tenants in receipt of benefit. The latter are assumed to be the poorest group. Data on health variables for council tenants as a whole are included for comparison. Controlling for income results in very small numbers of lone fathers in some cells.

First, the table shows the association between health status and socioeconomic status measured by housing tenure. Thus among men in couples and all women, council tenants have poorer health than home owners on all measures. Second, the table suggests that material living standards may be differentially associated with the health of lone parents according to sex. There

Table 4.4 Health of couples and lone parents by housing tenure and income amongst parents in single-family-unit households

	Couples				Lone parents			
	Mothers		Fathers		Mothers		Fathers	
	%	base	%	base	%	base	%	base
With long-standing illness								
home owners	22	(5938)	23	(5850)	25	(256)	35	(55)
council tenants:								
all	28		33		36		35	
no benefit	28	(2358)	32	(2314)	32	(219)	24	
with benefit	34	(426)	40	(428)	39	(424)	47	(34)
With recent illness								
home owners	11	(5935)	9	(5850)	15	(256)	11	(55)
council tenants:								
all	13		11		20		9	
no benefit	13	(2357)	11	(2315)	18	(219)	6	(34)
with benefit	15	(426)	14	(428)	21	(424)	12	(34)
Good health in previous year								
home owners	71	(5867)	78	(5546)	66	(252)	58	(55)
council tenants:								
all	57		64		46		50	
no benefit	58	(2334)	65	(2164)	52	(217)	56	(34)
with benefit	52	(425)	55	(421)	43	(423)	44	(34)
Poor health in past year								
home owners	7	(5867)	4	(5546)	7	(252)	13	(55)
council tenants:								
no benefit	12	(2334)	9	(2164)	15	(217)	6	(34)
with benefit	17	(425)	20	(421)	23	(423)	18	(34)

Source: GHS, 1980–82 for both couples and lone parents

appears to be no clear association between housing tenure and health among lone fathers to parallel that described among lone mothers, except that reported good health seems to be associated with home ownership. The disparities in recent illness between lone parents by sex are increased when tenure is controlled for. Lone mothers who are council tenants are more than twice as likely as lone fathers in council accommodation to have had RRI (20 per cent of lone mothers, compared with 9 per cent of lone fathers). On the other hand, the previously observed small excess of long-standing illness amongst lone fathers disappears among council tenants.

Taking account of income level within the council tenant group, it is apparent that overall tenure masks wide disparities. On all the health measures, women and men in the poorest circumstances (council tenants in receipt of benefit) report poorest health. Lone fathers in low-income households are twice as likely to report a long-standing illness as those in higher-income households (47 per cent compared with 24 per cent). Amongst the poorest group of lone parents, men report more long-standing illness than women, but amongst higher-income council tenants lone mothers are more likely to report a long-standing illness than lone fathers. Gender differences in reported good health are also smaller amongst lone mothers and fathers who are low-income council tenants than amongst those with higher incomes. This suggests that very poor living standards may be more strongly associated with a negative evaluation of health status amongst lone fathers than amongst lone mothers.

There is also some suggestion in the table that the differences in the health status of lone and couple mothers is greatest amongst those living in the poorest circumstances. This is contrary to the findings of other research, and could mean that lone mothers' experience of ill health is more strongly related to poor living conditions than is that of couple mothers.

In summary, then, it appears that differences in the experience of ill health between lone mothers and fathers reduce, the lower the household income. Part of the overall gender difference in health status amongst lone parents may thus be explained by the mothers' poorer socioeconomic circumstances. Among mothers, differences in the rates of reported ill health between women in couples and lone mothers widen as household income falls. This suggests that poverty entails a greater additional burden for lone mothers.

Social support and employment status

The GHS, being restricted to the household, is not the ideal source of data on kinship issues, but it can indicate the extent to which there may be social support within the immediate circle of the home. We cannot, however, determine the quality of the relationship between lone parents and other household members: the presence of other people in the household may be a benefit to a lone parent but may also represent an increased burden of caring, and in many cases both will be true (Qureshi and Simons, 1987).

One's position in a household is an indicator of stage in the individual life course, and may be closely related to age and marital status. Analysis of the GHS has shown that around 9 per cent of lone parents, mainly younger lone mothers, were living in their parents' home, while around 7 per cent, mainly (relatively older) lone fathers, were the heads of households which included other adults.

Table 4.5 shows how the health of lone parents differs according to whether other adults live in the household. There is some evidence that better health status is associated with living with others, for both lone mothers and lone fathers, though the patterns differ according to the health measure used. Lone fathers living with other adults appear more likely than those living with their children to report that their health has been good in the previous year, although they are also more likely to have a limiting long-standing illness.

On the other hand, lone mothers appear to be in better health when living with others. This may be linked to the fact that these women are likely to be younger never-married mothers. However, the strongest relationship is evident with regard to recent illness amongst lone mothers, reported by 18 per cent of those living alone and 10 per cent of those living with others. To the extent that this measure is picking up aspects of ill health that are less age-related than the long-standing illness measure, it suggests that the patterns described are not simply a reflection of age differences.

The data in Table 4.5 reflect a complex set of roles and relationships within the home, which cannot be disentangled using the GHS. We can, however, consider one important aspect of the social lives of lone parents – labour-market position – which may contribute to the patterns identified above.

Household composition and labour-market position appear to be related. Table 4.6 suggests that for lone fathers, living with other

Table 4.5 Health of lone parents by household type and sex*

Household Type	Alone %	Alone base	With others %	With others base	All %	All base
With good health						
male	55	(129)	70	(20)	57	(149)
female	54	(913)	53	(176)	54	(1089)
With long-standing illness						
male	35	(129)	33	(21)	35	(150)
female	32	(914)	26	(174)	31	(1008)
With limiting long-standing illness						
male	19	(129)	24	(21)	20	(150)
female	19	(914)	18	(174)	19	(1088)
With recent restricting illness						
male	11	(129)	14	(21)	11	(150)
female	18	(916)	10	(176)	17	(1092)

*Table includes lone fathers who say they are married and women whose husbands live away from home.
Source: GHS, 1980–82

Table 4.6 Employment status of parents* by household type (in percentages)

	Alone	With others	All parents
Mothers			
Employed F-T	25	22	17
Employed P-T	25	12	33
Keeping House	42	55	45
Unemployed	7	4	4
Non-employed	2	7	1
All (=100%)	(732)	(115)	(8046)
Fathers			
Employed F-T	71	75	89
Employed P-T	4	0	2
Keeping House	12	6	0
Unemployed	8	13	7
Non-employed	5	6	3
All (=100%)	(96)	(16)	(7155)

*Including parents in couples.
Source: GHS, 1980–81

adults may be associated with greater involvement in the labour market. They appear more likely to be in full-time employment and less likely to be keeping house than those living alone with their children. Lone mothers, on the other hand, are less likely to be in paid work, either full-time or part-time, and more likely to be in full-time housework, when other adults are sharing the household with them. This indicates that living with others may be a qualitatively different experience for lone mothers compared to lone fathers, and overall it appears to reinforce traditional gender roles.

According to Table 4.7, paid employment is associated with better health than non-employment amongst both lone mothers and lone fathers. About 62 per cent of lone parents in employment reported good health in the previous year compared with 47 per cent of those not in paid employment. This may therefore make our findings from the previous table more directly relevant to the health issue.

Being 'not employed' is mainly associated with full-time housework among women, but with unemployment, or non-employment because of sickness, among men. In consequence, 47 per cent of men who are not employed suffer long-standing illness, compared with 36 per cent of women in the same position. A different pattern occurs with regard to recent

Table 4.7 Health of lone parents by employment status and sex

Employment status	Employed %	base	Not employed %	base	All %	base
With long-standing illness						
male	29	(106)	47	(43)	34	(149)
female	26	(511)	36	(584)	34	(1095)
With recent restricting illness						
male	11	(106)	12	(43)	11	(149)
female	15	(513)	19	(586)	17	(1099)
Reporting good health in last 12 months						
male	61	(105)	47	(43)	57	(148)
female	62	(512)	47	(584)	54	(1096)

Source: GHS, 1980–82

restricting illness, however. Lone mothers are more likely to suffer RRI than lone fathers, and among lone mothers the highest incidence is among those who are not in employment. The data in this table do not take account of the type or hours of employment. Findings reported elsewhere suggest that these factors are important (Popay and Jones, 1988). Among lone mothers, reports of good health follow a clear gradient according to the degree of labour-market participation, ranging from 66 per cent of lone mothers in full-time employment, through 58 per cent of those in part-time work and 49 per cent of those in full-time housework, down to 31 per cent of the non-employed (see also Arber *et al.*, 1985).

Obviously, no causal inference can be drawn from these data, and it may well be that poor health is the reason for non-employment, just as employment may contribute to good health. Interestingly, the positive relationship between employment and reporting good health found for lone mothers does not hold for mothers in couples (Popay and Jones, 1988). Whatever the direction of causation, therefore, it is not uniform across parental groups. It is, however, likely that for some lone parents employment brings with it positive health benefits as a result of improved living standards, higher social status and greater access to support networks. The differences in employment status of lone mothers and fathers may thus explain some more of the gender differences in the experience of ill health.

DEMANDS OF THE CARING ROLE

We turn finally to consider the way in which the varying demands of the caring role may contribute to patterns of ill health amongst lone parents. There is evidence that these demands are greater for lone parents than for married couples, and that the nature and level of caring demands will be linked to the age and number of children. In couple households it is women who take the major share of caring responsibilities (Kowarzik and Popay, 1988). This situation may contribute to the poor health of lone mothers compared to married women. If lone fathers are experiencing similar caring demands to women, then the relationship between the scale and nature of caring demands and the experience of ill health should be similar for lone fathers and mothers, all other things being equal. If, however, lone fathers have fewer caring demands, then this might be a contributory factor in their relatively better health compared to lone mothers on all the GHS measures except long-standing illness.

Caring demands will increase when a child is ill, and may therefore have a more direct and visible impact on the health of parents. In order to explore this issue further, we considered the relationship between health of lone parents and that of their children. We derived a summary variable with which to describe the health of children and parents, so that intra-household health comparisons are possible. In Tables 4.8 and 4.9 we examine the health of parents in relation to the health of the sickest child in the family. This health variable combines long-standing illness and recent restricting illness. Where neither form of illness is present, health is described as good; where either or both long-standing illness and RRI are present, health is described as 'fair to poor'.

According to Table 4.8, children in lone-father households are more likely to be reported to be in 'good health' than children with lone mothers (78 per cent of children of lone mothers, compared with 86 per cent of children with lone fathers). On this summary health variable, lone mothers are more likely than lone fathers to have good health. (This is due to the combining of both long-standing illness and recent illness in these measures.) In all, 49 per cent of mothers who reported their children to be in poor health reported themselves to be in poor health, compared with 45 per cent of lone fathers.

Table 4.9 examines the relationship between having a sick child and the parent's likelihood of experiencing a recent restricting illness. Overall, 25 per cent of lone mothers whose children were in fair to poor health reported having had a recent restricting illness themselves, compared with only 10 per cent of lone fathers. Among lone mothers, there thus appears to be a clear association between the health of their children and their own experience of ill health. This is not apparently the case among lone fathers.

It could be argued that women (and men) in poor health will tend to report poor health amongst their children. Other researchers have tested this hypothesis and have argued that the

Table 4.8 Health of parent by health of sickest child (in percentages)

| | Health of child | | |
Health of parent	Good	Fair to poor	All
Lone mothers			
Good	72	51	68
Fair to Poor	28	49	32
Row percentage	78	22	100
Base	(917)	(263)	(1180)
Lone fathers			
Good	66	55	65
Fair to Poor	34	45	35
Row percentage	86	14	100
Base	(127)	(20)	(147)

Source: GHS, 1980, 1981, 1982

Table 4.9 Recent restricting illness of parent by health of sickest child, controlling for housing tenure

| | Health of child | | | |
Health of parent	Good %	Fair/Poor %	All %	Base
Lone mothers	15	25	17	(1184)
Owners	12	16	13	(306)
Renters	16	28	19	(870)
Lone fathers	12	10	12	(148)
Owners	12	(1)	11	(62)
Renters	12	(1)	12	(86)

Source: GHS, 1980, 1981, 1982

relationships they found could not be explained by such report-ing bias (Platt *et al.*, 1989).

The different socioeconomic circumstances of lone mothers and fathers may explain these gender differences, so we also control for housing tenure in Table 4.9. As can be seen, 28 per cent of lone mothers with children in fair to poor health living in rented accommodation had suffered recent illness, compared with only 16 per cent of home-owning mothers. Again, reliable comparison with lone fathers is not possible because of small numbers, but it appears from the table that housing tenure has less effect on the association between lone fathers' experience of recent illness and the health status of their children.

Table 4.10 presents similar analysis for the summary health variable described earlier, tenure. Amongst mothers in owned accommodation with children in poor health, less than a third (32 per cent) were themselves in poor health; amongst mothers in rented accommodation with children in poorer health, more than half (54 per cent) were themselves in poorer health. These findings support the argument that a sick child has a more detrimental effect on the health of lone mothers than on that of lone fathers, even under similar socioeconomic conditions.

Taking all the evidence together, it would seem reasonable to assume that some part of the difference is due to the fact that lone mothers experience more caring demands than lone fathers.

Table 4.10 Health of parent by health of sickest child (in percentages), controlling for housing tenure

Housing tenure		Owned			Rented	
Health of child	Good	Fair/ Poor	All	Good	Fair/ Poor	All
Health of parent Lone mothers						
Good	79	68	77	70	46	65
Fair to Poor	21	32	23	30	54	35
Row percentage	80	20	100	74	26	100
Base	(243)	(62)	(305)	(670)	(197)	(867)
Lone fathers						
Good	69	(4)	64	65	(7)	65
Fair to Poor	31	(6)	36	36	(3)	35
Row percentage	84	16	100	88	12	100
Base	(51)	(10)	(61)	(76)	(10)	(86)

Source: GHS, 1980, 1981, 1982

SUMMARY

Lone parents report themselves to be in poorer health on all the health measures available in the GHS than parents living in couples, and amongst lone parents there are sex differences in health which reflect the heterogeneity of this group. We suggested at the outset that the reasons for differences in the health of lone mothers and fathers lay in differences in their marital histories, in their socioeconomic circumstances, and in the nature of their roles as parents. Our findings from the GHS tend to support this view.

Where lone fathers are in poorer general health than lone mothers, notably in terms of long-standing illness, this appears to be due to their age and histories. Lone fathers are likely to be older than lone mothers, and more likely to have been widowed. Among marital-status groups, the lone parents reporting the poorest health are older men following their wives' deaths, and women who have become lone mothers after separation from their husbands.

On all measures except long-standing illness, the poor health of lone mothers compared to that of lone fathers stands out. They even have higher rates of long-standing illness than fathers in couples. There are considerable differences in the socioeconomic circumstances of lone parents: lone mothers are less likely to be in employment and to be home owners than lone fathers. They are also much more likely to be living on low incomes and in receipt of means-tested benefits. They therefore have fewer financial resources to help them with their roles as parent and provider for their children.

It appears that lone fathers have less daycare responsibility than lone mothers. Their children are older; they may be more likely to get help from others in the household. In contrast, many lone mothers have children under five, and only half of these have any arrangement for daycare, either formal or informal (Popay and Jones, 1990). The children of lone mothers are likely to be in poorer health than children in lone-father families, perhaps because they are younger and perhaps, too, because they live in greater poverty. It appears, therefore, that parenting demands on a lone mother tend to be greater than those on lone fathers.

In consequence, whilst most lone fathers are in employment, most lone mothers are full-time houseworkers. Since employment is the main means of escaping from the poverty trap, as well as providing other types of benefits, many lone mothers with young children are unable to improve their situations and may remain in a vicious circle of poverty and social isolation, from which they can escape only through marriage or when their children start school. In the meantime, their poor living situation is likely to take a considerable toll on their health, which may be reflected in their experience of morbidity and mortality in later life. Finally, social isolation may be an important contributory factor in the poor health reported by lone fathers and lone mothers.

Poverty and material disadvantage are major factors in the patterns of health and illness we have described. Improved access to paid employment, particularly for lone mothers, is undoubtedly part of the solution to lone parents' poverty, but this must mean improved provision of daycare facilities. Employment opportunities cannot be the whole answer, though, given the relatively low wages available to women. Income support will continue to be needed, at least until inequalities in earnings between women and men are reduced – a principle apparently accepted in many other countries (Millar, 1989).

It must not be forgotten that many thousands of lone mothers and fathers manage day after day to provide positive, loving and enjoyable environments for themselves and their children. What we have tried to show here is that in this endeavour lone parents may be paying a high price in terms of their health.

NOTES

1. The research was undertaken as part of the ESRC-funded programme of research within the Centre for Studies in Education and Family Health, an ESRC Designated Research Centre in the Thomas Coram Research Unit. We are grateful to OPCS and the ESRC Data Archive for the use of the General Household Survey; and to the parents who have taken part in our research. We are also grateful to Charlie Owen, the Senior Programmer at the Thomas Coram Research Unit, for his advice and assistance over the course of the project, and to Olwen Davies, the project secretary.

2. We have deliberately not included tests of statistical significance. This is for a number of reasons. First, we want to draw attention to the size of any substantively significant associations. Secondly, statistical significance is strongly influenced by sample size: some of our sample sizes are very large (e.g. couples) whereas others are small (e.g. lone fathers). Consequently relationships might appear to be present in the former and not in the latter, even when the effects are comparable. These issues are discussed in Morrison and Henkel (1970).

5 Income, employment, daycare and lone parenthood

Michael Hardey and Judith Glover

The main sources of household income for the majority of lone parents are social security, paid work, maintenance, or some combination of these. The dilemma that lone parents have to resolve is how to balance the generation of income with the demands of lone parenthood. The employment opportunities of lone parents are influenced by individual earning capacity and the accessibility of daycare. Social security forms an important part of the income of the majority of lone-parent households, and has to be taken into account when examining the employment strategies of lone parents. The age of the youngest child is the main factor which shapes the employment opportunities of mothers, whether lone parents or in conventional families, so that women who have pre-school children are unlikely to be employed (Haskey, 1986; Martin and Roberts, 1984; Weale *et al.*, 1984).

The term 'daycare' has been used in this chapter because 'childcare' has become associated with state intervention into families and the use of the Child Protection Act (Melhuishe and Moss, 1991). Most daycare in Britain is undertaken by mothers, but other members of the household, especially fathers, may also make an important contribution (Dex, 1988; Martin and Roberts, 1984; Yeandle, 1984). This daycare performed by fathers – referred to here as 'household daycare' – not only reflects gender divisions within the household but also influences the nature of much of women's employment. When household daycare is the only feasible option, women's employment has to be fitted in around its availability. Thus early-morning and evening work, which is typically unskilled, part-time and often insecure, may be the only form of employment accessible for many women with partners. Although it is difficult to establish a causal relationship, it is reasonable to assert that a major reason for women's employment in part-time, low-paid jobs or their non-employment is the lack of widespread, affordable, good-quality alternatives to household daycare. Lone parents who do not have the option of household daycare therefore face a major disadvantage in the labour market in addition to those faced by all women. Discrimination in the labour market lowers the average pay of women (Ermisch and Wright, 1989), further constraining their ability to pay for daycare. The employment rate of lone mothers in Britain compares unfavourably with that in France, as Baker's chapter in this volume shows (Chapter 6), and is the third lowest in the European Community (Cohen, 1990).

For women bringing up children, employment becomes more accessible when children are of school age. However, this is limited by school hours, school holidays, half-terms, child illness and similar constraints. Household daycare has the significant advantage of being unpaid so that the income from a low-paid, part-time job is not fully taken up with buying daycare, although it may involve reciprocal obligations (Finch, 1989). The implication for lone parents is that, faced with a lack of household daycare, they have to be reliant on relatives, or private or public provision.

The Family Expenditure Survey asked lone mothers of school-aged children who did not work whether they would work if they had access to daycare. Half of the women said that they would take up paid work (Millar, 1989). This is in line with evidence from a number of studies (Tivers, 1985; Weale *et al.*, 1984). As the Finer Report suggests, 'many lone mothers . . . are anxious to work' (DHSS, 1974, p. 412). The increased employment of married women has led to the recognition that even within a gendered division of labour in the home, parenthood and employment can be combined successfully.

Lone parenthood is still regarded by policy-makers as problematic, and this situation is compounded by the relatively poor material situation of most lone-parent households. The right of lone parents to be full-time parents supported by social security will remain important, especially when the household contains young children. Equally, the ability of lone parents to contribute to the household income and gain some of the social and other opportunities offered by employment is important. Many lone parents are so constrained by their circumstances and the restrictions of the labour market that their employment opportunities are confined largely to unskilled, low-paid, temporary or part-time employment (Millar, 1989; Weale *et al.*, 1984).

This chapter examines the employment of lone parents and its relationship to both daycare and social security. The background of daycare and the employment of lone parents is outlined and related to changes in employment and daycare patterns. Public and private provision such as workplace nurseries, childminders and nurseries are discussed, and the degree to which they can open up employment opportunities is assessed. The interplay between social security, paid work and daycare is examined, and some of the strategies developed by lone parents to reconcile their different demands are explored. Material is used from Hardey's recent in-depth research into lone parents to illustrate some of the themes in this chapter (see Chapter 3, this volume).

THE DEVELOPMENT OF DAYCARE

During both world wars, the demand for women to enter employment was sufficiently high that a widespread system of nurseries and other daycare provision developed rapidly. The recognition of the need for women's labour in World War Two was such that Ernest Bevin, when Minister for Labour, stated that it was 'a matter of first importance to the war effort' (quoted in Braybon and Summerfield, 1987, p. 106). Under this imperative the fourteen nurseries that existed in England and Wales in October 1940 had been expanded by the Ministry of Labour to 1,345 by July 1943 (Central Statistical Office, 1987). With husbands absent owing to the war, employed mothers were confronted by many of the problems of bringing up children alone that face lone parents. The daycare and employment dilemma was resolved by a national system of what was regarded as high-quality daycare and a general acceptance of working mothers. However, despite this high point in daycare provision, the state appeared to view the employment of women as a temporary and undesirable measure. The Beveridge Report made it clear that 'the attitude of the housewife to gainful employment outside the home is not and should not be the same as that of the single woman. She has other duties' (Beveridge,

1942, p. 51) – namely, caring for her children and making a home for the breadwinner.

At one level the loss of women to the labour force after 1945 opened up employment opportunities to demobilised service-men but the policy, as Mitchell points out, had an important ideological role: 'Instead of national workers they were to be private wives . . . in the effort to rebuild the family the equation went: delinquent = latch key kid = having been abandoned by its mother in infancy to creche or evacuation' (1975, p. 228). The interplay between prevailing psychoanalytical theories, employ-ment and the provision of daycare opportunities has always been significant. The work of Bowlby and Winnicott made the notion of 'maternal deprivation' the accepted wisdom of the growing social work profession. For the majority of families the end of the war appeared to present a return to prewar family life under the direction of the male breadwinner as 'head' of the household. However, the war also left many widows, children with absent fathers and a rising number of divorces. Widows were relatively well provided for by a pension to replace the husband's lost income. Lone parents had to be reliant on National Assistance if they had no other source of income, but under the prevailing notions of family and daycare they were treated as 'mothers first and workers second' (Lewis and Piachaud, 1987, p. 36).

Despite the rapid decline of a widespread national daycare system in postwar Britain, since the early 1950s there has been a growth in the economic activity of women with dependent children, albeit principally in part-time employment. During the past decade, the sharply rising level of employment for women has been associated with the rise of service-sector jobs at a time of economic restructuring such that the labour market has become segmented largely along gendered lines (Beechey and Perkins, 1987, p. 9). This increasing participation of women in the labour market has been accounted for in terms of changes outside the household – namely, demographic and economic factors such as the predicted fall in the number of sixteen- to nineteen-year-olds in the labour market between 1988 and 1994 (Department of Employment, 1989).

The Institute for Employment Research has forecast that there will be an increase in the labour force of just over one million between 1988 and 2000. Virtually all this increase is expected to be made up by the employment of women, because the sectors of the economy which are thought likely to experience the most rapid growth will be the service industries, in which most women are employed at present (Department of Employment, 1989). However, such predictions are made on the assumption of continued economic growth, which must be questioned as the economy enters a recession. The impact of a recession on women's employment is not clear, and its effect on lone parents is difficult to assess, but their level of employment is likely to be adversely affected by an increase in general levels of unemployment (Ermisch and Wright, 1989).

EMPLOYMENT AND SOCIAL SECURITY

Although there has been a marked overall increase in the employment of women, the employment of lone mothers has declined from 48 per cent of their number in 1979 to 39 per cent in 1985 (DSS, 1989). Cohen (1990) reports that there was virtually no increase in the employment of lone mothers between 1985 and 1988, in contrast to a general increase in the employment of women during this period. Fewer than 20 per cent of lone mothers and married women work full-time, but 36 per cent of married women (compared to only 24 per cent of lone mothers) work part-time (Millar, 1989). Lone fathers, however, are more likely than lone mothers to be employed, although relatively few work part-time (Haskey, 1986). It is the decline in part-time employment which explains much of the overall fall in the labour-market activity of lone parents.

The interaction between the social security system and paid employment goes some way to account for the low level of employment among lone parents. Layard *et al.* argue that

there is little incentive for a single mother to go out to work unless she is going to work full-time at a reasonable hourly rate. But . . . women's hourly earnings are much lower than men's. Thus the direct influence of low pay on poverty is probably greatest in the case of single-parent families (1978, p. 98).

Ermisch and Wright (1989) report that the average earned income of employed lone mothers is about 60 per cent that of the male average. One should add that the lack of daycare or the need to pay for it acts as a further significant disincentive.

There is a long association between lone-parent households and dependence upon social security (Marsden, 1973; Millar, 1989; Townsend, 1979). It has been estimated that nearly three-quarters of all lone parents were entitled to some means-tested benefits in 1985 (Berthoud, 1985), and a Department of Social Security report (DSS, 1989) noted that 43 per cent of all DSS expenditure on families was accounted for by lone-parent households. The 1986 Social Security Act followed a review of social security based on the government's belief that the social security system had 'lost its way' (DHSS, 1985). The reformed system was intended to be simpler, offer 'real' incentives to work and target resources towards 'genuine need'. Supplementary Benefit – which was claimed by over two-thirds of one-parent families in 1987 (HM Treasury, 1989) – was replaced by Income Support. As under the previous system, lone parents have a higher earnings disregard than other claimants, but Income Support takes no account of work expenses such as daycare and travel to work, unlike the benefit it replaced. At the time of writing, lone parents can earn up to £15 per week before they suffer a concomitant loss of benefits. This represents a real loss in terms of the value of the earlier disregard for most lone parents who have to meet daycare expenses (Brown, 1988). The income supplement for those employed full-time with a low income became Family Credit. Like the previous Family Income Supplement, the take-up level of this benefit may be small (Brown, 1983; Davis and Ritchie, 1988). Families in receipt of the new means-tested benefits remained entitled to Housing Benefit, but a steeper taper for rent/community charge rebates was introduced, and all claimants have to contribute to water charges.

The implementation of the 1986 Act represented a fall in the real income of long-term claimants and did not generally restore benefits to their value at the beginning of the decade (Brown, 1988). 'Transitional protection' was given to those transferring from the old to the new benefits to maintain their standard of living. It should be remembered that non-means-tested Child Benefit and One-Parent Benefit have retained their real value over the past decade. These benefits are significant to individual households, as they provide a regular and reliable income

(Millar, 1989). Lone parents who receive means-tested state benefits face a social security/earning 'plateau' which they may have to take into account when considering paid work. Broadly, any earnings over the £15 disregard will make no actual contribution to household income and can under some circumstances lead to a drop in household income due to the loss of social security benefits and/or related benefits such as free school meals (Ermisch and Wright, 1989). Joshi (1987) has suggested that a lone parent would have to have an earned income of more than £125 per week in order to add to the overall household income. This points to the existence of a poverty trap (DHSS, 1974; Hurstfield, 1978) that is hard to overcome when lone parents may face wage disadvantage (Joshi and Newell, 1987) and need to take account of daycare costs. It should be noted that the research that is drawn on in this chapter was carried out after the 1986 Act was implemented.

Separation and divorce form the principal route into lone parenthood, so maintenance can be a source of household income, but for lone parents dependent on social security it cannot currently contribute directly to the overall income of the household. Maintenance can be collected by the DSS, to help offset the cost to the state of supporting lone parents on social security, but the cost of collection and default is high and is reflected in the low level of maintenance collected by this route (Edwards and Halpern, 1988). Maintenance contributes in a significant way to the household income of only about 6 per cent of lone mothers (Millar, 1989); this reflects both the difficulties of collecting the payments and the inability of many absent partners to provide adequately for two (or more) households. However, it has a strong symbolic significance if it is seen in the light of 'parental responsibility' and the retention of 'traditional values'. The right-wing Centre for Policy Studies regards fathers who default on maintenance as 'contributing to the breakdown in authority' in society, and 'abdication of men from fatherhood' is viewed as a significant factor in the 'decline of family life' (*The Guardian*, 23 April 1990). For those lone parents who are not dependent on social security and receive a reliable and significant amount of maintenance, it is an important part of the household income. For the majority of lone parents who are wholly or partly reliant on social security, the contribution made by maintenance to the household income is insignificant.

PUBLIC PROVISION OF DAYCARE

The rise and decline in the public provision of daycare and the increase in the part-time employment of married women have been outlined above. For many married women part-time work is possible because they have access to household daycare and do not have to be reliant on other forms of daycare. However, while household daycare may support part-time employment, it will not support full-time work and its contribution to holiday care is variable (Yeandle, 1984). Thus all lone parents and many women in two-parent households have to be reliant on daycare outside the home.

Local-authority nurseries provided places for under 1 per cent of all children under four in 1985 (Cohen, 1988). They now offer an essentially residual service for children considered to be in 'special need' due to the disadvantaged situation of their family. Under this definition lone parents have access as priority users. Should a lone parent wish to use such a nursery, however, access to places is not automatic and is subject to waiting lists. The desire of a lone parent to take up paid employment is frequently not seen as a legitimate claim on a public nursery place. This can be seen in operation in the experience of a lone father who had worked part-time in his old job while his younger child went to nursery every morning:

> I had to give up going into the garage every morning to work when the nursery told me that I could only be sure of a place three mornings a week. I explained that I was keeping my hand in at work but the manageress told me that the nursery was there to help the children and the parents, not so they could leave them to go off to work. I think she was angry with me because I didn't join in any of the activities for parents as I was at the garage.

Following the 'social problem' orientation of these nurseries, many, as Cohen (1988) notes, have become the focus of family centres geared to the 'needs' of disadvantaged families.

Local authorities can also provide schemes for school-aged children considered to have 'special needs'. Several state-supported schemes linked to special programmes,, such as the Department of Health's Under Fives Programme, have developed as a result of the Children Act 1989. These provide daycare for a relatively small number of children, defined by their 'social problems'. However, access to publicly funded daycare on these terms is likely to become stigmatised (Cohen, 1990). Jane, a never-married mother who lived on a large inner-city estate which had a local-authority nursery, explained why she did not wish to use it:

> The nursery is for people who have got problems. I could get Gemma into it as I'm a single mother but I don't want to get involved with the people there. This is a rough estate and you get all sorts down there. I don't want to be associated with that. Once you get in there the welfare people think they have a right to poke their noses into your life because they think you can't cope. If there was a better nursery I would use it because I could get some kind of work while she was there and she would like to play with the children.

The prevailing attitude to the direct involvement of the state in daycare can be seen in a statement from Edwina Currie, then Junior Health Minister: 'Our view is that it is for parents who go out to work to decide how best to care for their children. If they want or need help in this task they should make appropriate arrangements and meet the costs' (cited in Cohen, 1990, p. 35). This approach is also followed in the area of taxation, which does not make any allowance for daycare costs, which are regarded as an 'item of personal expenditure' (cited in Cohen, 1988, p. 16).

PRIVATE PROVISION OF DAYCARE

The private provision of daycare, which is mainly made up of nurseries, childminders and playgroups, accounts for less than half of all daycare for working women (Martin and Roberts, 1984). For pre-school children, nurseries and day-nursery schools can provide care between nine and five o'clock. Playgroups tend to offer fewer possibilities for working parents, as they are often available for only a few hours a week. Children of all ages can be cared for by childminders, many of whom may be unregistered (Cohen, 1988) and thus unquantifiable. Parents must pay for private-sector provision, the cost of which is very likely to be prohibitive for many on low incomes.

Cohen notes that the majority of children who are cared for by childminders are there in order to allow parents to work (1988,

p. 27). They can offer a greater degree of flexibility than most other forms of daycare. One advantage is that the same childminder can look after young children, provide after-school care for older children and holiday care for both. They may also be more accessible for parents who are restricted to public transport in their travel between home, daycare and work. Childminders and parents have a one-to-one relationship which is centred on the home-based care provided by the childminder and develops beyond a simple purchaser–service-provider relationship. The arrangements are personal in a way that distinguishes the relationship from more institutional forms of care. As Sarah, who had a four-year-old daughter, said:

> I prefer the childminder to the nursery because she can cater far more to my child's needs. There are only three children with her and they get on like a little family. She is also far more flexible than the nursery. I can arrange to pick Sophie up late if I need to and she does not charge if Sophie is ill.

Even so, this one-to-one relationship and the sense that the childminder is doing a 'good turn' can have disadvantages (Brannen and Moss, 1988). Mary felt that she was caught between her sense of obligation to the childminder and the demands of her eight-year-old son:

> It is a difficult situation. He is picked up from school with the childminder's children but they don't get on very well. It is hard because she is a lovely person and we get on well but Sam says the children pick on him. I try and get friends to pick him up but I can't rely on them for every day. I don't want him to go home on his own as I don't get in until six. So it is a difficult problem and I can't afford to fall out with the childminder as I have to rely on her.

The cost and quality of childminders vary considerably, but in general they are cheaper and more flexible than nurseries (Brannen and Moss, 1988; Cohen, 1988). As a home-centred activity which can embrace the care of the minder's own children, it can also provide employment for some lone parents. Yvonne, a nursing sister, who had tried to carry on working after a divorce, described how she became a childminder:

> I have always nursed but I found that I could not cope financially after being on my own for two years. With three children my

daycare bill left me very little to live on. I had sometimes to work
shifts and so I had to get sitters in to put them to bed. I felt their lives
were being disrupted. Childminding was an obvious alternative
and it can fit in with my children. I miss going out to work and
nursing but I am better off and of course have more contact with my
own children.

WORK-BASED PROVISION OF DAYCARE

The increased demand for women to become actively engaged in
the labour force has given renewed attention to the workplace
nursery. While the workplace nursery accounts for only a very
small proportion of all private daycare (EOC, 1989), it has the
advantage of locating working parents and children close
together and being geared to parents' working hours. This is
important to lone parents who are unable to rely on the support
of a partner to share daycare tasks such as taking and picking up
children from their daycare.

The end of the 1980s witnessed an upsurge in publicity for
workplace nurseries as some employers faced with recruitment
problems set out plans to provide nurseries for employees. For
example, the Midland Bank was prominent in promoting its
plans to establish up to 300 nurseries, but by the end of 1990 it had
established only three nurseries of its own, although places were
purchased at other nurseries (Incomes Data Services, 1990).
Some employers, such as hospitals, have also set up nurseries in
order to help retain or attract skilled women in health-care work.
Here cost is a crucial factor, especially for the relatively high
proportion of women workers employed in the public sector. A
survey of 120 employers in the private and public sectors
reported that only four offered assistance with daycare costs
(*Industrial Relations Report and Review*, 1989). Some London
schools under ILEA provided subsidised nursery places. Penny,
who taught in a primary school adjacent to a public nursery,
described the benefits of such a scheme and the opportunity it
opened up for her:

I carried on teaching after my husband left. I went part-time for two
terms but the twins liked the nursery. As it was subsidised I could
afford to use it while I worked full-time. Teaching does not pay very

well so I could not afford a childminder and the nursery was next to the school.

The costs of a workplace nursery may be prohibitive to many lone parents and other potential users who do not earn enough to pay the fees. The demand for unsubsidised places seems likely to be confined to relatively well-paid and skilled employees.

In countries with a developed daycare policy, such as France, employees have long since voiced their preference for local provision over that of employer-based daycare (Phillips, 1989). While it appears unlikely that a significant number of workplace nurseries will be developed in Britain, it is worth relating the experience of one lone mother who had returned to work after having her baby:

> There is a nursery there. It is not cheap but the care given to the children is very good. I don't have much more to live on than if I was unemployed after it's been taken out of my salary. What gets me down is that I have no hope of moving on in my job. I've got to stay at this branch because I will still need the nursery for another year or so. I have not been able to get any promotion or go on training courses because I would have to be able to move to another branch which I obviously can't do.

It may be in the interests of employers to provide workplace nurseries, which tend to lock employees needing daycare into dependence, encouraging what David and New (1986) refer to as the 'tied-cottage syndrome'.

Despite the lack of information about the nature and extent of workplace nurseries (Cohen, 1990), employer initiatives appear deficient on several counts. Workplace nurseries are in any case confined to larger employers, so that parents employed in small concerns have few of their daycare needs recognised. The Equal Opportunities Commission has proposed a national daycare development agency which would be funded by an employer levy (EOC, 1990). Similar schemes funded by contributions from employers, such as the *Caisses d'Allocations Familiales* in France, have helped provide good-quality care and brought a higher proportion of lone parents into the workforce (John Baker, this volume, pp. 110–25). Rejected by the Confederation of British Industry and out of tune with current government non-interventionist policy, such schemes would seem to stand little chance of success in Britain. In addition the CBI has stated that the large-scale expansion of workplace daycare is unlikely, preferring to see flexible working hours as its main strategy for encouraging women to return to work (*The Guardian*, 25 April 1990).

Employer-based daycare provision provides an example of the attachment of benefits to the worker rather than to the citizen. This is in line with recent trends in Europe, where the Third European Community Action Programme on Women has explicitly changed its terms of reference from a series of measures – including high-quality daycare – aimed at the citizen to measures aimed at the worker. The long-term results of this trend could lead to a two-tier system composed of, on the one hand, parents in paid employment for whom daycare may be available, and, on the other hand, parents who are outside paid employment, for whom these resources are unlikely to be either available or affordable.

OUT-OF-SCHOOL PROVISION

The needs of school-age children are not often considered by employers beyond the creation of flexible working hours and employees' normal entitlement to holidays. While flexible working arrangements help to reconcile the daycare/work dilemma, they fail to resolve the problem of school holidays and child illness. It is difficult to estimate how many children regularly look after themselves after school or in the holidays. What is apparent is that children of all ages are left to supervise themselves and sometimes care for younger siblings (Petrie and Logan, 1986; Simpson, 1978). This practice is by no means confined to lone parents; it also shows up the weakness of household daycare where both parents are employed. Children outgrow not only nurseries but also other forms of daycare such as childminders. The ages and circumstances under which children are left to care for themselves vary greatly, but parents come under increasing pressure from children to move away from formal care arrangements. Ken, who worked full-time, described how his daycare strategy changed as his children grew older:

Gareth is twelve and has resented going to the minders after school because there were only young children there. I suppose I also thought about the money I would save if I didn't use the childminder. He goes home after school and is there for a couple of hours until I get home. He knows that he must phone me if anything goes wrong and my neighbour would help out in an emergency. But I can't help worrying about him. He sometimes goes round to friends after school if it has been arranged but I will not allow him to have them round at our house unless I am there. He thinks this is very unfair and we fall out over it occasionally in the holidays.

There is a link between the willingness of a parent to adopt a self-care strategy and the environment in which they live. The stigma attached to children labelled 'latchkey' can combine with a concern about children left on their own in neighbourhoods viewed as unsafe. This dilemma was expressed by a lone mother who left her part-time employment during the school holidays so that she could supervise her two children:

It is not that I don't trust my own children but the estate is not a safe place for them to be on their own. It would be a constant worry to me if they were here alone. I can't afford a phone and the boxes around here get smashed up so they would be unable to ring me.

A range of play and holiday schemes is organised by local authorities, voluntary groups or employers, or run as private enterprises. Many of these do not aim to provide daycare as such, but rather activities for children during the school holidays. The extent, cost and quality of such schemes are difficult to assess. A London-based study noted that lone parents were frequent users of playschemes (Petrie and Logan, 1986), but this may be due to the association of such schemes with relatively poor urban areas which tend to have a high concentration of lone-parent families (Haskey, this volume, pp. 40–3). The hours such schemes operate are often not sufficient to enable a parent to use them as a major source of daycare, but they can be part of a complex juggling of daycare during the holidays. In two-parent families, household daycare may play an important role in providing holiday care (Yeandle, 1984). In theory ex-partners could support lone parents by providing daycare in such circumstances. In practice this appears to happen only rarely, despite the attempts of some lone parents, like Ruth, to include ex-partners in a package of holiday care:

> I dread the summer holidays. My 'ex' always says he will take the kids off my hands for a week but when it comes to it he never has. So I have to get help from my parents and friends. Luckily I have a friend who is also on her own and our children are about the same age. She doesn't work and looks after all the children some of the time. My two go to the sports centre twice a week where they can have sports lessons and then one or other of them may go and visit a school friend. It takes a lot of organising and there are times I have to take a day off because there is no one to look after the children.

The difficulties of arranging regular, good-quality daycare in the holidays can in some areas lead to the strategy of entering and leaving employment in line with school holidays. Helen found that she could easily find work in shops, which she left every summer:

> I used to pack my jobs in every summer so I could fit in with the school holidays. I only did them to get some extra money so I wasn't very fussy about what I did. I never earned very much, not so the social [security] would know.

However, this is possible only in areas where there is a high demand for labour. In addition it leaves lone parents locked into low-paid jobs without any of the rights of permanent employees.

Employers may not recognise absenteeism due to a sick child as legitimate, and compared to many European countries parental rights under employment law in Britain are limited. Child sickness can be a major problem because no daycare provision – apart from household daycare, nannies and other live-in care arrangements – can easily provide care for unexpected child illnesses. While for two-parent families the extent of household care in the face of illness is questionable (Yeandle, 1984), lone parents have to rely on help from outside the home or take time away from work. Friends and relatives who live nearby can be pressed into service during the occasional child illness, but as Heather – who had been employed full-time for three years – found, they cannot be used for longer periods:

> I had a good job in a design office but Rebecca went down with measles and was quite ill for six weeks. My mum helped a bit but

she is getting on and has to take care of my dad. I felt that it should be me who looked after her but I could only take a week of my holidays off work. I could not go to work so I got the push and have been at home ever since.

EMPLOYMENT, INCOME AND DAYCARE STRATEGIES

Employed lone parents have to develop a strategy that enables them to reconcile the demands of employers and children, especially in the shape of daycare. In addition, they need to provide extra household income which is frequently under-written by a contribution from means-tested social security benefits. The calculation of the benefits of working are complex and not simply economic. Even if considerations were confined to the issue of maximising the household income, levels of knowledge about the range and interrelationship of means-tested benefits available make it unlikely that purely economic decisions can be made (Bradshaw, 1989; Martin and Roberts, 1984; Popay *et al.*, 1983; Sharpe, 1984; Weale *et al.*, 1984). Wage-support benefits such as Family Credit tend to be under-claimed (Davies and Ritchie, 1988). Some lone parents mistakenly believe that they are breaking social security or housing benefit rules by being employed. Sandra described how her employer 'kept quiet' about her part-time job, from which she earned about twelve pounds a week at an hourly rate of about a pound:

> I work in a shop four mornings a week and get paid in cash so that there is nothing to affect my social [security payments]. It's a favour to me you see because I'm not supposed to be earning. I have to get some extra money. I can't live on just what I get in benefits and I can be earning while the children are at school.

Sandra had devised a strategy which increased the household income, but it hid the way she was being exploited. Similar lack of knowledge and a concern not to risk an established household benefit income (Millar *et al.*, 1989) can make lone parents unwilling to move from Income Support to Family Credit, which would involve making a new claim based on evidence from an employer. A shift to a wage-supplement benefit can take place only when daycare and work strategies have been developed. As already noted, the direct cost of daycare diminishes as the age of the youngest child and the possibilities of self-care increase. Linked to a concern expressed by some lone parents about a future when their children become independent, the move into full-time employment can be a significant transition. Mary had two children and had worked part-time as a clerical officer since she became a lone parent. She faced this kind of choice:

> I could go full-time and after a while take some training and exams which I have been offered. My present job is very basic, you know, routine, but my boss wants me to get on and be able to use my initiative more. I'd love to do something that is more of a challenge. . . . Now the children are older it is not so necessary for me to always be at home after school. . . . At first I wouldn't earn that much and I'm worried that I'd lose out on benefits to the extent that I could not afford to carry on. I need to think about my future before the children leave home so if I could afford it I would take the chance.

Opportunities for promotion, training and a career are relatively rare in the area of the labour market occupied by most lone parents. Few employers recognise that part-time, often un-skilled, work can be a stepping-stone. Significantly, Mary was employed in the public sector by an employer who had an active equal-opportunities policy which had the potential to work to her advantage. Thus the job that a lone parent occupies can be important for the potential it offers for training and promotion. Lone parents may be able to take full advantage of such opportunities only when their daycare needs and costs decrease as their children grow up.

Training has become a recognised route into work for the unemployed, women returners and lone parents. Courses to encourage lone parents' participation in the labour market have been funded by the EC Second Poverty Programme and targeted at areas with a high proportion of one-parent families. However, local labour-market conditions and the demands of daycare form a considerable barrier to satisfactory post-course employment (Hyatt and Parry-Cook, 1990). Since 1987, lone parents (unlike married women) have been able to receive a daycare allowance of up to £50 a week on some government-supported training schemes. The schemes last for only a year, after which no further state subsidy is available, so that it is possible for lone parents to be financially worse off if they accept low-paid full-time employment (Slipman and Hadjipateras, 1988).

More traditional forms of training offered by further and higher education are sometimes supported by subsidised daycare resources. Part-time day education can provide courses targeted on women with children, and a few colleges have subsidised nursery places. The daycare itself can be the initial attraction to non-working lone parents as a 'break' and later become a stepping-stone into a career. Gillian is one of the few lone parents who has followed this route, and she described how it had led to higher education:

> I went to the day classes really to have a break from the children when they were young. The crèche was free so I did a couple of courses and one which was linked to the Polytechnic. I always thought I was not bright enough for real study but I enjoyed the course and I was asked if I wanted to do a degree. I remember that I didn't think this was possible but they were very good to me and found out all about grants and courses I could do to fit in with the children.

This route into employment is potentially the most dramatic, as it can transform the position of unqualified lone parents into one where they can command more than adequate earning power. However, the relatively low real value of student grants and the increasing costs of education mean that it may become an even harder route for lone parents in the future.

Full-time employment presents the greatest hurdle to lone parents, especially if they have children under five, and this is reflected in the low level of full-time employment amongst both lone parents and all mothers with young children (GHS, 1985; Martin and Roberts, 1984). As Haskey (this volume, pp. 34–8) shows, lone fathers are relatively older, have fewer and older children and are more likely than lone mothers to be in full-time employment. Their higher rate of employment is partly accounted for by these characteristics, but it also reflects the segmented nature of the labour market. It is dangerous to apply generalities to lone parents as a broad category (Crow and Hardey, 1991), and this is also true of groups within that category, such as lone fathers. Millar (1989) notes that there is greater polarity amongst lone fathers than lone mothers in terms of household income, and this reflects an overall division between the circumstances and income of those employed and those who are totally dependent on social security (George and Wilding, 1972; O'Brien, 1987).

Full-time employment can provide sufficient income to overcome many of the difficulties with daycare that lone parents encounter. Nannies and boarding-school education provide daycare services for affluent lone parents. A lone mother who decided to have a child on her own and to return to her job in financial services explained how she resolved the problem of daycare:

> I made a clear decision to have Jane on my own. I had an established career and was well able to provide for a child even if the father was not involved. I took a year out and then got a nanny. I work at home sometimes and I don't think that Jane misses out because I work. On the contrary she has many more adults and children in her life than she would in an ordinary family. My colleagues who have children all have nannies or send the children off to boarding school so I don't think Jane misses out on anything.

There is little information about the extent or form of daycare by nannies or *au pairs* (Cohen, 1988), but its high cost precludes it as an option for the majority of working parents, especially employed lone parents.

Lone fathers' household responsibilities may not be recognised by employers, particularly those in predominantly male occupations. This may mean that a conventional career will suffer because there is no partner support or because the employer's expectations are such that the demands of daycare cannot be met. Jeffrey worked in a national bank and became a lone father when his two children were still in primary school:

> I think my career has suffered because I am a sole parent. . . . You could say that I lead two very different lives, one in the bank and one at home. At the bank it's quite usual for people to take work home and I can be quite flexible in my working hours. What I can't do now is to join in the social life or be able to take up assignments that would take me away from home overnight. . . . There are things that should be done to get promotion and I can't do these, which goes against me.

Jeffrey was able to introduce a degree of flexibility to his working arrangements, but felt that there was a cost in terms of his own career.

Occupations like the construction industry, based on traditional expectations about domestic divisions of labour, can greatly disadvantage lone parents. George had established himself as a self-employed builder because he could not work in a conventional firm after he became a lone parent with responsibility for two children under ten:

> I was working for a local firm but I could not put the hours in that were wanted. They wanted me to work weekends and evenings at short notice and I couldn't arrange for the children to be looked after to do that. Setting up on my own means that I am in control of the jobs I do and so it is easier to sort the children out when I am working.

There is evidence to suggest that self-employment is a more common strategy than part-time employment for lone fathers (Haskey, 1986); this may reflect the gendered nature of much part-time employment.

Job-share schemes, flexitime and shift work may provide the flexibility required by lone parents. Diana was able to undertake full-time shift work because her mother undertook part of the role of household care:

> I have to shoulder all the responsibility which means that I work because it's the only way we can survive financially. I do office cleaning late at night while my mother comes round to babysit. I'm lucky because I don't have to pay her anything to come round and I can catch up on my sleep when the children are at school and be at home when they come out.

Lone parents have developed diverse employment strategies which change as the demands of the household change. In some cases these strategies will become part of reconstituted two-parent households, or other household forms. They are flexible and constantly reconstructed in order to reconcile the conflicting demands of household and labour market. However, the ability to develop these strategies is constrained by the resources and demands of lone-parent households. Expensive daycare such as nannies and other live-in arrangements came closest to replicating the role of household care, but the cost makes this option beyond the reach of most employed lone parents.

CONCLUSION

Lone parents' access to the labour market is more restricted than that of men and women in two-parent households because they lack the resources of household care. For the majority of lone-parent households, social security makes a vital contribution to the household income. The complex interrelationship between benefits, other welfare payments and any earned income has to be part of an individual's strategy for combining employment and daycare. Maintenance payments are significant only for the minority who receive them on a regular basis and for whom they make a positive contribution to the overall household income. The earnings disregard figure of Income Support acts as a barrier to many lone parents dependent on social security actually contributing more to the household income by working. This barrier is reinforced by employment-related costs, principally daycare, but it may also involve travel costs, which can effectively take up a large proportion of an earned income. Part-time employment strategies are therefore more complex for lone parents than for parents in couples, particularly as the majority of these do not have to take account of the social security system before the economic consequences of employment can be assessed.

Ex-partners appear to play little active part in supporting the employment strategies of lone parents and are not able to replicate the role of household care. While relatives and kin can make an important contribution to daycare in some lone-parent households, the majority are dependent for regular employment on resources outside the home. The public provision of daycare has become largely residual and although lone parents in suitable locations are potential users, their use of such facilities is defined in terms of their needs as 'problem families', not as consumers of daycare. Market-led daycare fails to offer an adequate level of employment opportunities because of its low availability, high cost and relative neglect of the need for out-of-school care. Work-based daycare provision is only rarely subsidised to any significant degree and can confine the employment opportunities of parents to one employer. Childminders can make an important and sometimes flexible contribution to employment strategies, but the individual arrangements are frequently *ad hoc* and the quality of care is variable.

Flexible employment practices and the recognition by employers of the constraints of lone parenthood can be important, particularly in the context of relatively poor employment protection and parental rights. Training and education have the potential to bring lone parents into the labour market, especially if daycare is recognised as a primary need, but they may provide only a tantalising taste of employment unless the local labour market provides jobs with sufficient income to support viable employment–daycare arrangements.

6 Family policy as an anti-poverty measure

John Baker

'Temporal analysis suggests that the family is tending to evolve in the same direction everywhere,' wrote the Italian team reviewing changes in the family for the EC (Comitato Italiano, 1982). This did not mean, of course, that family structures are yet the same. The team noted continuing differences between 'rural' and 'urban' families and, related to this, different family structures in the various European countries. They put Britain, France, Germany and possibly Denmark in one group, furthest along the line in which evolution seemed to be taking place. In these countries families were small, a high proportion of adults – and especially wives – were in employment, the proportion of young heads of households was relatively high and there were many households containing just one adult. The Netherlands, Luxembourg and Belgium had some of the same characteristics, but the distinctive patterns of Ireland and Italy seemed to be crumbling.

Researchers specifically looking at one-parent families have also come to the conclusion that there are common patterns. Roll wrote: '. . . it is striking the extent to which all countries [of the European Community] have experienced the same trends' (Roll, 1989, p. 2). O'Higgins said the same, adding that there is no sign that the number of one-parent families has yet reached a peak or plateau (O'Higgins, 1987). Kamerman and Kahn (1988) talk of 'mother-only' families as a universal problem for the industrialised world. It is clear, too, that a further common theme for one-parent families is poverty, or at least relative economic disadvantage. This is a conclusion of all the texts cited, and many other national studies on one-parent families – for example for Britain (Millar, 1989) and the several countries reviewed in Deven and Cliquet (1986), Smeeding *et al.* (1990) and, for France, Villac (1984).

These comparisons and trends are, of course, broad ones.

Precise comparisons are difficult. Measures and even definitions vary. There is no obvious agreement, for example, on what should be counted as a one-parent family. It is obvious too that it is a far from homogeneous category – the situation and experience of widowers will have little in common with that of 'schoolgirl mothers'; the proportion of different types of one-parent families differs in the various countries, and the provision for the difficulties encountered by superficially comparable families may have little in common.

This chapter concentrates on one comparison – Britain and France – but attempts to put that comparison into a wider European context. Both countries were considered by the Italian team to be among those furthest along the line of development that other countries appeared to be taking. There are many common features between the two. The characteristics of one-parent families are similar, as are their situations in law as far as child custody, attitudes and maintenance are concerned. However, there appear to be significant economic differences. One-parent families are worse off than others in both countries, but the gap would appear to be significantly smaller for most such families in France than it is in Britain. The contrasting outcomes from similar starting-points may produce lessons on how to reduce the poverty of one-parent families and their children; in particular it might throw light on the policy options identified by Kamerman and Kahn (1988).

The plan of the chapter is to show the broad comparability of the nature and origins of one-parent families in Britain and France. Both may be examples of what might happen elsewhere. Then it contrasts the economic position of such families in the two countries. It then attempts to explain this difference – French family policy clearly has a major role. However, French one-parent families are not greatly helped by the relatively few cash benefits and concessions 'targeted' either on them or on 'the poor'. They gain substantially – and often to a greater extent than other types of family – from provisions intended to help all parents, all women and all families, and in particular from childcare provision allowing mothers to work. Then there is a discussion of why France has a different and stronger tradition of family policy, and whether there are any lessons from this for Britain and other countries. In policy terms, the comparison reinforces Kamerman and Kahn's judgement that the British policy supporting poor mothers at home leaves them badly off, but that a combination of a wider family policy with an appropriate labour-market strategy appears to offer better prospects. The issue, however, is how to get sufficient political will to make the necessary changes.

ONE-PARENT FAMILIES IN BRITAIN, FRANCE AND OTHER COUNTRIES

The long-standing French political concern with demography has meant that family patterns and behaviour are fully researched, although census data – from 1982 – are now somewhat old in an area where change is rapid. Policy-relevant information has been summarised in Laroque (1985), *Données Sociales* (especially 1984, 1987) and is updated regularly in the official commentary on social data, *Economie et Statistique*. As far as one-parent families are concerned, trends are sufficiently similar to Britain's that one has to look elsewhere for the explanation of the greater relative prosperity of one-parent families in France.

In the early part of the postwar period the number of one-parent families was falling. The principal cause was death, and death rates among people with children in their charge were falling. Mothers died as well as fathers. Most one-parent families were female-headed, but this was far less the case than later. Widowers commonly continued at work. For them, money was less of a problem than daycare. Widowhood was sometimes an insured social security risk. Where there was no social security – especially in rural areas or in the small-business sector – there were sometimes extended families or inheritance to act as a cushion. Wealth in France was and is more widely spread than in Britain (Centre d'Etude des Revenus et des Coûts [CERC], 1979).

A turning-point in the number of one-parent families became evident in the 1968 census. Death continued to decline as a cause of one-parent families and became a relatively minor one – although still the major cause of father-headed ones. From the late 1960s onward there was an accelerating growth of one-parent families from the causes found in Britain and most of the 'advanced' world – separation, divorce, and a growth of motherhood outside marriage. This last phenomenon is as difficult to interpret in France as it is in Britain.

Clearly there is an element of the 'welfare mother' stereotype – young, poor, demoralised girls getting pregnant – but only a small one. Obviously sexual behaviour had changed, but so had the ability not to get pregnant or have a baby. Modern methods of contraception became available throughout most of France when they did in Britain and abortion, in a mainly private health system, was readily available even before it was liberalised in 1975. Many never-married mothers had clearly made a choice: they were older, more prosperous and better qualified. Some were certainly on their own, some with parents, but some were clearly cohabiting (or had involvements) with the father. As in Britain, about half of 'illegitimate' births are jointly registered, with a high proportion of parents giving the same address, but it is difficult to know what the relationships between parents and children are. Probably, 'juvenile cohabitation' is prolonged into parenthood without a formal ceremony (Audirac, 1986; Desplanques and de Saboulin, 1986; Rallu, 1982a; Villac, 1984).

These trends are common between the two countries and others (Meulders-Klein and Eekelaar, 1988). Before French figures are considered, the divorce, child custody and mainte-nance law will be outlined because, for all the emphasis on parenthood outside marriage, it accounts for only one-sixth of one-parent families. Widowhood, separation and divorce account for the rest.

Family law in France is broadly similar to Britain's and not dissimilar to that in most Western countries except Ireland (Meulders-Klein and Eekelaar, 1988). In 1975 most 'matrimonial fault' grounds for divorce – though not necessarily the attitudes – were swept away. There can be divorce by consent and – unilaterally imposed after a delay – for 'rupture of conjugal life'. Separation and divorce rates have, as in most comparable countries, risen enormously. Most 'broken' families are 'recon-stituted' by remarriage or cohabitation, and most single mothers form a relationship with a man – the younger the mother, the more quickly. Hence many more families will have gone through a phase of single parenting than are in it at any one time.

These points are familiar to students of British family life. French figures – mostly taken from *Données Sociales*, 1984 and

1987 – show that in 1982 there were not far short of a million one-parent families containing 2.5 million people, out of a total population of 53 million. Ten per cent of families with children were one-parent ones, constituting 6 per cent of all households. They contained 9 per cent of children. Half of one-parent families arose because of divorce or separation, a third from death and a sixth from parenthood outside marriage. Five-sixths are female-headed. Taking trends from 1968 to 1982, lone parenthood resulting from death fell by nearly a quarter, from separation rose by a tenth, from motherhood outside marriage rose by 170 per cent, and from divorce rose by 220 per cent. One-parent families tend to be smaller than others. Half have only one child, but this and other features vary quite sharply according to how people become lone parents.

The probability of becoming a lone parent – and, of course, remarrying – varies according to stage in the life cycle. Four out of five single mothers have only one child, often a young one. The family size of the other types of family does not vary very much, but divorced mothers are fractionally younger, with younger children than widowed ones (Rallu, 1982b). Figures produced by O'Higgins (1987), Millar (1989) and Roll (1989) indicate that most urbanised and industrialised countries of the world show – or are starting to show – similar patterns, with variations according to their special features – for example the illegality of divorce in Ireland and the continuation of rural extended families in Italy.

THE RELATIVE PROSPERITY OF FRENCH ONE-PARENT FAMILIES

One-parent families appear to be better off in France than in Britain, both absolutely and relatively. The first is, of course, to be expected, given the generally poorer living standards of the British compared at least with the original six members of the European Community. The French may be on average some 50 per cent better off, according to Gross National Product per head. The relative prosperity may be more interesting, given that in other respects French income may be less equally divided than the British (CERC, 1979), despite ragged recent moves towards greater equality (Kessler and Masson, 1985).

However, before coming on to the greater relative prosperity of French one-parent families, there are clearly qualifications to make. French one-parent families are still disadvantaged over money, housing, daycare, social isolation and other signs of deprivation. Their children are more likely than others to have to repeat years in school, and one-parent families – widows excepted – are much less likely to be owner-occupiers (Le Gall and Martin, 1987; Rallu, 1982b). They are particularly likely to have to move house once or several times (Boudoul and Faur, 1987; Taffin, 1987). A minority of one-parent families may be markedly worse off than in Britain, because of the different social security systems. In Britain, Income Support is comprehensive and fairly easy to claim. It is a safety net which allows few people – and certainly few one-parent families – to fall to even lower standards of living. French social security may provide better benefits to most claimants, but it does not have the same safety-net function. Where it does, 'constituting the dossier' can be long and complex, leaving people, including one-parent families resorting to it, with little or nothing – apart from discretionary payments, loans or charity – for short or long periods. *Aide Sociale* – the safety net – is residual and has largely disappeared except as a means of paying medical bills for the indigent. For those who receive it it is local, a loan, subject to family means tests, discretionary and a contribution only to-wards food, or even bread alone (Verdier, 1984). There is a more generous *Allocation de Parent Isolé* (One-Parent Benefit) but it affects only some 7 per cent of one-parent families. None the less, most French one-parent families seem to be better off than their British counterparts.

A major survey in 1978 compared the incomes and other features of different types of family in France (Villac, 1984). The national average income per 'consumption unit' in households was given an index of 100. The unit of consumption is a crude attempt to standardise living standards across different sizes and types of household. The first adult counts as 1, a second or a child over fourteen counts as 0.7, and other children as 0.5. The index of the standard of living per consumption unit in two-parent families varied, by age of the 'head', from 89 to 95. Lone-father households generally had higher-than-average standards of living, ranging from 97 to 109. Lone-mother households ranged from 68 to 89. Sixty-eight is a low score, but it was for separated women, a small group often in a temporary predicament. The figure for the largest group of one-parent families, those headed by a divorced mother, was 79. For other types of one-parent family the index varied between 75 and 89. Interestingly the highest score, 89, was for single mothers. This was exactly the same as that for two-parent households with a 'head' aged under thirty, probably the group with which they would most naturally be compared.

Since these figures were collected there has been a considerable relaunch of family policy. In 1981 family benefits were substantially increased, then allowed to slide back again somewhat, but some were then increased again (Laroque, 1985; Liaisons Sociales, 1989, 1990). The gap between all families and the rest of the population must have closed, some one-parent families benefiting especially from the extra help given to mothers of young children.

There can be no precise calculation of comparable British figures. There is no series of figures with 'equivalence scales', with two exceptions. Historically, many British sources have compared household incomes with Supplementary Benefit scales for families of different compositions. This precludes any international comparison and the 'equivalence' for children is low compared with the French calculations. Even these figures are no longer published. There are now figures which purport to show how one-parent families compare with others, but the source contains no details of how 'equivalence' is calculated (DSS, 1990). There are also figures for gross and net incomes of one-parent households and how these compare with other types of household, but these are of very limited use without equivalence calculations, given how different one-parent families are in size and composition from other sorts of household.

However, such data as do exist render unbelievable the idea that many British one-parent families enjoy even the two-thirds average income that was the lowest figure for France, let alone the four-fifths enjoyed by the biggest group. Taking, first, Supplementary Benefit scales (now Income Support), at the time of the Family Finances Survey (Knight, 1981; Millar, 1989), over half of all one-parent families living on their own had incomes within 10 per cent either way of Supplementary Benefit scales. Only three in a hundred had incomes 40 per cent or more above.

Eekelaar and Maclean's sample (1986) were marginally more prosperous, but only 8 per cent enjoyed what they called an 'average family' standard of living. The large and growing gap between social security incomes and earnings has been copiously documented, for example in Walker and Walker (1987). The scale rate on social security for single parents in 1978, for example, was only 18 per cent of average male earnings – a gap so enormous that additions for children and housing costs could never have remotely closed it. For a single person under twenty-four the figure in 1989 was 10 per cent (Department of Social Security, 1989). Using the new DSS equivalence scales (whatever they may mean), a quarter of single parents had less than half average incomes after housing had been paid for, and half less than 60 per cent. Only one in six had an average income or more (Department of Social Security, 1989). British one-parent families are clearly less well off.

A comparison of social security entitlements is interesting. Social security is the principal or exclusive income of most British one-parent families. In France the *Allocation de Parent Isolé* is one of the few 'safety-net' benefits. In theory all pregnant women or sole parents should have their income brought up to this level if it would otherwise be below. Despite the fact that it is considerably higher than Income Support, only some 7 per cent of French one-parent families receive it. The following are July 1990 figures:

Table 6.1 Social Security support in Britain and France (in £ Sterling)[1]

	Allocation de Parent Isolé[2]	Income Support (exclusive of housing costs)
Pregnant woman (18–24)	55.44	28.80
Parent (over 18) with one child under 11	74.16	60.50
Parent (over 18) with 2 children under 11	94.11	72.85

Notes:
1. £1 = 12.63F – the purchasing parity equivalent calculated by CERC (1979). The market exchange rate is approximately £1 = 10F, which would make the difference seem greater.
2. French benefit rates, July 1990.

Another area of comparison is the effects of divorce. According to a 1980 survey of divorced women in France, only a minority (38 per cent) felt that their standard of living had fallen. Nearly as many (31 per cent) felt that they were better off. Eekelaar and Maclean (1986) have looked at the effects of divorce on British women. They talk of 'exceptional adversity' suffered by lone parents following a divorce, with four out of five of those who had not found a new partner being below their poverty line. The questions posed were not the same; none the less, there is a stark contrast.

The last area of comparison is poverty studies. Again there can be no exact comparisons. The French have no tradition of poverty studies compared with the British and use different tests in the few studies that have been done. Franco-British research has found one-parent families in France only slightly more likely to be in 'poverty' as they defined it than two-parent ones, but much more so in Britain (Mitton and Willmott, 1983; Smeeding *et al.*, 1990). Hauser and Fischer, analysing 1979 data for Britain, reported 31 per cent of the smallest one-parent families and 56 per cent of the largest as having less than half average net incomes. Figures for France in 1975 quoted by O'Higgins (1987) indicate 23 per cent of French one-parent families as having less than half average incomes. Again, the methodologies are not strictly comparable, but the differences between the situations of one-parent families in France and Britain are very large.

The French 'poverty studies' that have been done are little more than exploratory (Debonneuil, 1978; Pascaud and Simenon, 1987). One-parent families do not feature strongly. British studies do not appear to bear out the French suggestion that only a few one-parent families are among the poorest 5 per cent of the population.

WHY ARE FRENCH ONE-PARENT FAMILIES BETTER OFF?

Three main sources of income go to one-parent families: maintenance from ex-partners, social security and wages. The role of all three is debated in both countries, but in Britain the first seems to get priority political attention and the last the least.

The relatively better position of French one-parent families is the result of better maintenance only to the extent that the money paid benefits the mother rather than, as in Britain, being deducted from social security income. That happens in France only to *Allocation de Parent Isolé* claimants. Maintenance is nevertheless only a modest additional contribution to the incomes of one-parent families – worth about 13 per cent of their income, according to Roll (1989). The figure is not higher for two reasons: court orders are frugal and payment is incomplete. The sums awarded by the court vary widely, but the commonest sum for 1980 was £50 per month from husband to wife as an adjustment of income, and rather less for the support of a single child (Meulders-Klein and Eekelaar, 1988). However, only 35 per cent of these orders are paid fully and promptly, and 13 per cent are never paid at all. There may be scope in both countries for boosting payments from fathers to one-parent families, but clearly this difference cannot contribute much to an explanation of the differences between Britain and France. However, the French, who now have a system of 'advance payments', have encountered similar difficulties in getting more money out of fathers as may be anticipated in Britain. Defaulters are difficult to trace, have little money or produce good reasons for not paying; not all mothers want to pursue the matter, and small, erratic civil debts are not easy to collect.

French social security benefits and tax benefits are not particularly generous to lone parents either. Several benefits and concessions are aimed at encouraging people to have more children, targeting families of three or more. For example, the *Allocation Parentale d'Education* pays up to £211 per month to mothers who give up work to have a third child, and there is a guaranteed minimum income for such families. Even the standard child benefit starts only with the second child – although they get £47 per month – and more still is paid for third and subsequent children and older ones. The tax system also privileges large families by dividing taxable income by a formula (*le quotient familial*) which reflects family size, and gives an extra 'point' to one-parent families. Hence large – or, better still, large and prosperous – one-parent families may do well, but there are very few such families. Most one-parent families are small and of modest means. Other benefits, however, may be of more use – the *Allocation au Jeune Enfant* (young child benefit) and the *Allocation Logement* (housing benefit).

The *Allocation au Jeune Enfant* is a regular payment of £68 per month for nine months around the birth of a baby, but extended until the baby is three for families of below-average income. This often dovetails with employment law and pre-schooling to enable a mother to keep a job. The housing allowance is too complex to give even meaningful illustrative figures. It is aimed not only at helping particular sorts of households but at financing house building and improvements, but some one-parent families benefit.

Eighty per cent of French lone parents work, nearly all of them full-time. It is this, combined with supporting and complementary legal social security and maintenance provision, that explains their comparative prosperity. Moreover, the jobs performed by lone mothers are 'normal' ones rather than the marginal, semi-casual ones – with appropriate wages and conditions – which most British lone parents do. The occupational distribution of French single mothers is much the same as for other working women. For example, 22 per cent of divorcees are in manual work, compared with 20 per cent of all women; 30 per cent are in office work (31 per cent); 5.3 per cent are senior staff (5.9 per cent) (Villac, 1984). French women tend to be bunched in two types of work – routine manual and routine non-manual – but to a lesser extent than in Britain. Fifty-eight per cent of workers on the minimum wage are women, compared with 42 per cent men – a significant difference, but probably less than would be found on a British definition of low pay. Further, gender differences in pay are falling in France but growing again in Britain (Benveniste and Lollivier, 1988).

The reason for this rate of employment is a highly developed system of daycare and pre-schooling. Pre-schooling is practically universal for children of three or over – 94 per cent go to school, the balance being almost entirely in rural areas where the number of one-parent families is negligible. Over a third of two-year-olds attend a nursery school. Taking children under three, 11 per cent are in school, 5 per cent in officially approved subsidised crèches, 8 per cent with 'official' childminders – only slightly over half are with their mother full-time.

There are good grounds for assuming that 'official' provision of substitute daycare for a quarter of babies covers most one-parent families where the mother seeks to work, though this does not mean that there are not particular difficulties in some cases.

Anecdotally and informally one hears many stories of how hard it is to get a nursery place and about the pleading, wheedling and cajoling necessary to find one, but most of them seem to have happy endings – something turns up or has been found rather than a job offer lost. However, this pressure could be successful only in the context of a policy to encourage daycare.

There are immediate and longer-term reasons for the availability of daycare. The immediate reason is often the role of the Family Benefit Funds (*Caisses des Allocations Familiales*). Family Benefits are administered on a local basis, albeit within a tight national framework. The local committee – consisting of employers, trade unionists, elected representatives of users and Family Association representatives – has discretion on how to spend a proportion of the contributions they collect from employers on services for children and families. This gives a local source of funds which may be spent on daycare facilities. As important as direct *Caisse* provision are joint projects. Pressure from the *Caisses* and their affiliate bodies results in services provided and/or funded jointly by the *Caisses*, employers, local authorities and voluntary bodies. Places in these nurseries or crèches may take need into account. One-parent families benefit as a by-product of services intended to help all families, all children, and working mothers.

Policies for combining daycare and work would, of course, be useless without work opportunities. There are special provisions in France to help the employment of women, and mothers in particular, which are of special benefit to one-parent families. Jobs must be kept open for mothers for two years. This, of course, bridges the period from advanced pregnancy until the age of the baby at which nursery places are generally available. It is also the period for which the *Allocation au Jeune Enfant* is paid. Mothers do not have to give up their place in the job market. In addition, parents have an absolute right in large organisations and a qualified one in small ones to have unpaid holidays or to go part-time for up to two years. This again keeps mothers – and especially single mothers – in jobs. Also of considerable help is the public sector. The state is an enormous employer. The public sector tries to lead society in matters of social attitudes, and this includes provision for parents. Most employees, including senior ones, are women. A substantial proportion of women 'at risk' of becoming single parents are found there: others gravitate towards it. There are modest wage supplements to parents working for the state (Fournier, 1989). By contrast, British public-sector employment is more gender-segregated than other employment.

WHY DOES FRANCE HAVE A STRONGER FAMILY POLICY?

French one-parent families appear to be better off than Britain's as an indirect and probably unintended result of policies aimed at helping women, children and families generally. The main driving force behind those policies appears to be the wish to increase the birth rate, by reducing the difficulties working mothers have in rearing children.

Historically, the reasons for the French wanting an increased population were economic, military and religious (Baker, 1986). Economically, France has always been portrayed as capable of supporting a larger population than it possesses. There has always been spare agricultural land, and until the 1970s there was never a national unemployment problem – both of which are linked in popular attitudes (if not in economic theory) with desirable population size. Military reasons (the ability to recruit soldiers) led even the arch anti-interventionist Napoleon to offer to take over the entire support of every seventh son born to a couple, provided he joined the army. The military reasons for population policy probably reached a peak in the interwar period and became irrelevant only with nuclear weapons. Catholic enthusiasm for large families does not always produce a family policy, but in France it did, and even today many attitudes to children seem to be secularised versions of religious beliefs. All these factors operated in the opposite direction in Britain. A high population relative to land and cyclical unemployment gave credibility to the theories of Malthus. Militarily, threats to Britain's naval supremacy meant that having a large population to feed was the threat. The Protestant religion has emphasised discipline in procreation.

Today these differences have become largely irrelevant, although the traditions have acquired their own momentum.

One is left with contemporary economic and political arguments. French economists and most British ones who have studied the question argue that in most circumstances the best long-term policy for rising standards of living is modest, steady population growth (Sauvy, 1969; Simon, 1983). In France the indicator used is that couples ought on average to have 2.4 children. This spreads the burden of the elderly. It keeps demand buoyant. Perhaps most important in the eyes of French economists, it provides a supply of new entrants to the labour force without which the existing pattern of economic activity will stagnate. Family policy is not something to be financed if resources permit. In Britain social policy is regarded as a consumption expense. In France it is regarded as an investment. Expenditure on it preceded the French economic boom and is seen as one of its causes.

The second argument is political. In France, family policy is popular. For example, only 4 per cent of the population in 1982 thought family benefits were too generous, two out of five thought benefits were too low, and nearly three-quarters wanted mothers of large families paid a wage (Bastide *et al.*, 1982).

The popularity of family benefits may be for traditional reasons, but there are other factors. Family provisions are on a scale that makes them of real help. The sums involved are such that even middle- and upper-class parents feel they have an interest in them. Most French people, like British people, have been, are, or intend to be parents They identify with provisions that help them. Family policy mitigates the crash in the standards of living that would otherwise occur when children arrive, with all the expense involved plus, possibly, loss of a wage. French academics appear amazed that in Britain the state is happy to see children reared during an economic trough in their parents' life cycle. Ordinary people seem amazed that the British public are not concerned about the drop in income that occurs when they become parents. Finally, there is the electoral support of women. French feminism is an ill-documented area, but impressionistically there is less 'American-style' feminism with its ambivalence and at times hostility to the family, and there appears to be a much more deeply structured concern about women's rights, including social policy to enable them both to take paid work and to have children.

THE POLICY RELEVANCE

Kamerman and Kahn (1988) identify four main types of policy response to one-parent families – an anti-poverty strategy (Britain), a categorical strategy (Norway), a universal young child strategy (France, Hungary, Austria, Germany, Finland) and a family policy and labour-market strategy (Sweden). They note, of course, that while poverty is a common problem for one-parent families, economic issues are not the only ones. It could be held, for example, that mothers ought not to take paid work but instead provide full-time care and love, at least for young children. Their own preference seems, however, to favour mothers retaining contact with the world of work, lest (among other things) they have problems when childrearing is over. Hence packages which combine work provision with other measures appear to appeal most.

This author would disagree with Kamerman and Kahn's classification of France, in that they appear to underemphasise the labour-market aspect of French policy. It could be more precisely labelled universal young child and labour-market policy. It appears, from the comparison with Britain at least, to be far more successful on the economic front than the anti-poverty strategy adopted here. The question, then, is: might such a strategy win support in Britain?

The 'demographic time bomb' – the decline in the working population compared with the old, and a predicted shortage of labour – appears to have been discovered in Britain very recently. French commentaries on other countries have highlighted this feature of Britain's future for about twenty years, and the French's own policy of modestly increasing the birth rate for themselves has had the avoidance of this as an objective for much longer (Laroque, 1985). An ageing population can be a vicious circle, for a short-term response to it may be to stimulate the employment of married women. Unless that is combined with daycare policies, the birth rate may fall again.

Daycare policies are necessary not only to enable mothers to work but to enable workers to have children. When Norman Fowler and others, reviewing social security arrangements in 1984 and 1985, panicked about the demography of pensions provision, their solution was to cut pensions. It should have been to improve daycare. The links between the two are not often made and the fault lies, ultimately, with academics. British demographers and social policy students do not often talk to each other, let alone to politicians. Since the issues are not politically obvious, there will not be a public debate before there is an intellectual one.

The second lesson from France is a political one. French family policy has a broad base. It appeals to all women, all parents and would-be parents, and all income ranges. Broad-based alliances are being sought in Britain, but lobbies have historically tended to be more narrowly based – defending the interests of the poor, or one-parent families, for example. The broad base would appear to be the more promising strategy. With the 'demographic time bomb' it could now include business, which in France has always backed a strong family policy.

7 Becoming a lone parent

Maggie French

The diversity of lone-parent households is a common theme running through the chapters of this book. A good deal of this diversity arises from the variety of ways in which it is possible to become a lone parent, ranging from death of a partner to the deliberate choice of 'going solo' (Renvoize, 1985). Most common of these routes into lone parenthood is the ending of a marriage through separation and divorce, where there is also considerable diversity in the processes of becoming a lone parent.

This chapter is based on one such route into lone parenthood, that where some wives married to men who 'come out' as gay after several years of marriage become lone parents. Contrary to common-sense perceptions this is not inevitable, but one mode of 'situational adjustment' (Becker, 1970) to the disclosure of a shift in a husband's sexuality. Numerous people become lone parents when marriage ends (Hart, 1976). Married couples divorce for diverse reasons, including adultery (Lawson, 1989) and marital violence (Brailey, 1985). Divorcees generally proceed through a lengthy process of 'uncoupling' (Vaughan, 1986). Many people pass through various stages in their adjustment to the sexuality of their partners. Some may renegotiate their marriage contract, accommodate a husband's gayness and maintain a two-parent family. Consequently, they create an alternative lifestyle. Others may adjust differently and become lone parents. An analysis of the experiences of those in my study illustrated the more general point that becoming a lone parent was not a single event. A sequence of stages was located when, in an interactive process, some women became lone parents gradually. It is this process that will be the focus of this chapter.

Many men do not develop a gay identity even if they are aware of same-sex attraction, because of the stigma attached to homosexuality (Plummer, 1975). Some think that the attraction will disappear if they develop a heterosexual relationship (Troiden, 1988) and many who marry assume that marriage is a confirmation of a heterosexual identity (Coleman, 1985). Some of the husbands in my study had been aware of and had revealed to their wives their pre-marital doubts about their sexuality. Notwithstanding, it had been assumed, in interaction with the social definitions surrounding marriage, that being married was a validation of heterosexual identity. The couples had not expected the gay identity to emerge after marriage, and both husbands and wives expected to live 'happily ever after'. After meeting a woman with whom they formed a close relationship, the men wanted to get married and build a family life. Their future wives had found someone they felt they could be happily married to. It is not impossible or even rare for gays to be fathers, nor are they likely to father gay children (Miller, 1979).

Whether or not they had been aware of the gayness before their marriage, neither partner had expected a shift in sexual identity after their wedding day. Some wives, who were aware, believed that 'love conquers all' (Brownfain, 1985) and had assumed that once married with children they would lead a conventional life. However, unexpectedly, after a period of marriage and family life, the husbands began to question their sexual identity and, for diverse reasons, 'came out' to their wives, in the context of heterosexual marriage. Emerging from this disclosure was an interactive process when the individuals negotiated and adjusted their lifestyles and identities. During this process most contemplated separation and/or divorce, though not many adjusted in this way. Some did, and became lone parents.

An analysis of the experiences of those in my sample who did become lone parents reveals that the fathers were not 'absent', for – as Harris (1983) and Rimmer (1983) found in relation to divorced parents in general – they were still involved in family life. Lone-parent households do not necessarily imply lone-parent families (Millar, 1989). Unlike the majority of lone parents, those in my study were not financially dependent on state benefits. However, they were constantly confronting and adjusting to diverse problems, constraints and opportunities, and employing various strategies in the process of becoming lone parents.

THE STUDY OF MARRIED GAYS

Between 1980 and 1984 I was in contact with a self-help group for the wives of gays. During this time I collected data from many members of this group and some others whom I met through introductions, who were not members. They were middle-class people living 'ordinary' middle-class lifestyles in different parts of Britain and working in various types of jobs. All were parents and had the same sorts of problems that any other parents experience. Overall they could be anyone's next-door neighbour, but because of the homosexual taboo these families tended to lead hidden lives which sometimes led to separation and divorce (Bryant and Wells, 1973). But to know simply that people are divorced and lone parents masks their experiences and the strategies they employ in the process of becoming lone parents.

The sample was not representative of all types of marriages and parents, but the interpretation of the data does support an interactionist analysis of the dynamics of becoming lone parents which is not untypical of the ending of marriages more generally. This type of analysis was developed by Blumer (1969) and illustrates how social life is in a constant state of flux and that, contrary to common-sense perceptions, sexuality is not static but constantly changing (Plummer, 1975; Weeks, 1986). So, too, is marriage. Both sexuality and marriage are shaped in interaction with social definitions and self-definitions. Similarly, being a lone parent is not static but an ongoing interactive process. It is an identity that is always emergent.

Although there were differences in the 'vocabularies of motives' (Mills, 1972), an analysis of the 'accounts' (Scott and Lyman, 1968) given by parents in the research revealed an emergent pattern of stages or phases where the various individuals were confronted with a set of problems to overcome. Individuals, in their interaction, are constantly faced with problems that need to be solved. As each problem is solved, another arises. Each solution leads to some form of negotiation, change and adjustment in the behaviour and identity of the individual (Plummer, 1975). Consequently, becoming a lone parent can be seen as a problem-solving course.

Influenced by the classic work of Davies (1963), an anlysis of the cycle of events which emerged in the relationships of some of the people in this study identified four stages. First, 'getting married and having children', when the couples meet, marry, have children and expect to lead a conventional life. From this stage they shift to the second, 'keeping the family together', when both partners are confronted with an unexpected shift in the husband's identity. Some consider, but resist, getting a separation and/or divorce. Following this stage they may shift to 'anticipating the future', when the parents negotiate the implications of the disclosure for their future lifestyles and identities. They may shift back to an earlier stage or proceed to the next. This fourth stage is 'coping alone', when each parent is confronted by the need to cope with living a life apart yet still in contact with their former partner. In an interactive process they create new identities and lifestyles. In this model people do not automatically shift from one stage to the next. Some may hover between phases and/or return to an earlier stage. As in other comparable situations, much depends on the individuals' interpretations and meanings of the events and the coping strategies employed (Fagin and Little, 1984; Mills, 1985; Murgatroyd and Woolfe, 1982).

GETTING MARRIED AND HAVING CHILDREN

Between 90 and 95 per cent of people get married, and 35 per cent of all marriages are remarriages for one or both partners (Central Statistical Office, 1989). People's motives for marrying vary (Gittins, 1985; Mansfield and Collard, 1988), but by marrying one's normality is confirmed. Many gays marry, and they do so for diverse reasons (Ross, 1983). These reasons reflect the social significance and privilege placed on 'compulsory heterosexuality' (Rich, 1980). In interaction with the taboo surrounding homosexuality and the social definitions of heterosexual marriage, many men and women assume that marriage is a validation of heterosexuality.

Some of the men in my study had been actively involved in the gay world before marriage, and some revealed their gayness to their wives before they married. The wives who were aware did not anticipate that the disclosure would be problematic once they were married. Most got married because they were 'in love' and had expected to lead a 'normal' heterosexual married life.

Regardless of their reasons for marriage or their awareness of the gayness, the partners in the study overwhelmingly defined this first stage of 'getting married and having children' as normal and conventional. Most relationships started as friendships that gradually became closer and eventually blossomed into marriage. In this they are probably no different from any other ways in which couples meet and marry (Mansfield and Collard, 1988). As time passed they had children. Some pregnancies were planned, whilst others 'just happened'. One couple, who had wanted children for some time, adopted a brother and sister. Most settled down, like many other families, into a 'conventional' lifestyle. They had similar problems to other couples, including financial difficulties and learning to cope with the day-to-day adjustments of living together and bringing up children. The expectations and redefinitions of sexuality that may take place during this stage can be seen in the experience of James, who explained:

> I'd only met one other girl before Christine . . . and we had a physical relationship but I didn't find it very good really. With Christine it was very good and when it worked well I thought well, I'm normal after all you see. . . . I decided I wanted to travel the world. . . . So we took off together. . . . It worked well so we thought it was a good basis for a marriage . . . we were very happy. . . . We came home here and got married for our parents. I felt a bit like Christine; we had been together for two years and felt comfortable together and it worked quite well.

James and Christine settled down into a 'comfortable' marriage and became involved in various activities and pastimes. After the first few years their sex life dwindled – this is not rare in conventional marriages (Greenblatt, 1983). James assumed that his marital relationship was the same as that in all heterosexual marriages:

> Neither of us was that interested in sex I suppose. I mean, I never saw it as being, well, I thought this is it when people are married and thought that their sexual life was different. But it [the marriage] was quite comfortable. . . . We used to go away at weekends . . . and most evenings we spent together. We both went to an evening

class. We used to see our parents and visit friends . . . . Looking
back it sounds rather nice now actually!

In her account of this stage Christine described how becoming
parents changed the marriage:

> We didn't know if we wanted children or not. I came off the pill and
> we decided that if anything happened we would accept the
> consequences. We weren't having much sex then. It did slow down
> a bit after we married. Two years later I was pregnant which was a
> blow to both of us. The baby turned our marriage upside down. . . .
> All the time I was pregnant James went off sex completely. . . . I had
> a miscarriage two and half years later. Then I became desperate for
> another child. Being an only child myself I wanted more than one.
> Eventually I conceived again.

In interaction with the social definitions surrounding heterosexual marriage, couples like James and Christine assumed that
being married with children meant that they would lead a
conventional heterosexual lifestyle. However, in the next stage,
the husbands disclosed their shift in sexual identity. Emerging
from this unexpected event was a state of flux. Both partners
were confronted with a situation they had not anticipated. The
relationship and their identities as heterosexual marrieds with
children were hurled into a process of change.

KEEPING THE FAMILY TOGETHER

In this stage identities and relationships were whirled into chaos
after the disclosure of the shift in the husbands' sexuality.
Although most conventional marriages change after the honey-
moon period and the birth of children, it was the need to confront
a shift in sexual identity that many blamed for the changes and
difficulties that arose in their family lives. They felt bemused,
confused, guilty and unhappy at the situation. Many developed
rationalisations for their marital difficulties and wished to maintain their marriages and identities as husbands, wives and
parents.

Different strategies and techniques of neutralisation are employed by many people whose behaviour is defined as socially
deviant (Ferraro and Johnson, 1983; Mills, 1985; Scully and

Marolla, 1984; Sykes and Matza, 1957). By employing neutralisation techniques the interactants shifted the definition of their
situation from 'something unusual' to 'nothing unusual' (Emerson, 1970). Emerging from this process, some of the couples
renegotiated their marriages and identities. They kept the family
together and avoided separation and divorce.

James felt guilty about the changes in his marriage that
followed the disclosure of his sexuality. However, these changes
did not lead to a rejection of his perceived responsibilities as a
father. As he said:

> It seems to be a fairly common pattern that the gay thing comes out
> when the children come on the scene. . . . If there hadn't been any
> children I might have gone off. It does concern me that we don't
> have much time together as a family. . . . The problem is that I
> don't see the family lives of other people and I think if anything
> goes wrong with the children and I think they're not getting a fair
> share of our time I think that it's because of the gay problem and
> that it's my fault.

Although he wished to pursue his gayness, James still wanted to
maintain his role and identity as a husband and father. However,
he felt that he was not giving enough of his time to his children,
which led to further feelings of guilt. Even though there are
diverse forms of fathering (Seel, 1987), James said he had limited
knowledge of 'the lives of other people' and could not compare
his family life with that of other contemporary fathers. However,
he employed a neutralisation technique by comparing his role as
a father to that of fathers in times past. As he explained:

> I think the guilty feeling is my own. I don't think they find it as bad
> as I imagine they do. Daniel is always out with his friends but Susan
> is still young. I suppose children never have seen a lot of their
> fathers in previous generations.

Miller's (1979) study revealed that many gay fathers are
concerned about their children's well-being. James wanted to
maintain his role as a father and felt that it was important to set
aside time to be with his children. As he described:

> I try to make an effort to do something with them every weekend.
> But it is the time problem. I like to see Joe [gay friend] on Sunday

mornings. . . . I'm still studying, and spend one day a week with
my mother. I feel the children lose out really. . . . But it's just that
there's something else in my life, it could be perhaps golf or another
male that I go out drinking with. . . . We normally have super
holidays together. I find that on holiday I do listen to the questions
they are asking. This year I'm taking the kids camping with a friend
and his children. . . . I do enjoy the children despite my moaning
about them.

Consequently, it is clear that although James's sexuality had
shifted, he still wished to maintain his identity as a father. This
was expressed in his concern that his children should not be
affected by the changes in his marital relationship.

Whether or not women are aware of their husbands' sexuality
before marriage, their initial responses to the disclosure when
married ranged from wanting husbands to leave the home,
through a willingness to renegotiate their marriage contract, to
ignoring the gayness entirely. Some blamed themselves and felt
guilty; they experienced a sense of isolation, shock, anger,
disbelief and a lack of self-esteem (Gochros, 1985, 1989). Most of
the women in this study felt bewildered about their role and
identity as a wife and mother and were concerned about their
children and family life.

Christine, like many women, neutralised the significance of
her husband's gayness:

The sexuality bit didn't worry me at all, but the fact that he loved
somebody else. That really got to me. The reason I married James
was that at long last I had someone to share my life with, which I
suppose all human beings long for – someone to share a life with
and never be alone again. Suddenly I realised I was to be alone
again because there was somebody else he wanted to be with more
than me. And that was the dreadful hurt. . . . It wasn't really the
sexuality because that hadn't been important in the relationship
anyway.

Not only did Christine fear loneliness if she and James separated,
she was also concerned about the effect of a divorce on her
children. As she said: 'Then of course there were the children, an
eight-week-old baby and a three-year-old child. I thought,
"Crumbs, they're going to be victims of a broken marriage", and I
didn't want them to be that.'

A coping strategy employed by many wives of gay husbands is

to seek outside help (Coleman, 1985; Gochros, 1985, 1989; Matteson, 1985). Christine contacted a gay agency to neutralise her feeling of 'being the only one in the world'. As she said, 'I cried a lot the next day and phoned *Gay News*. I thought I cannot be the only woman in the whole country. There must be somebody else. I must reach them – how are they coping?'

Emerging from this strategy, Christine became a member of a self-help group of wives married to gays. In interaction with other members of this group she became aware of how others had negotiated the situation and variously adjusted their identities, family lifestyles and relationships after the disclosure. Many couples, like Christine and James, renegotiated their marriage contract and adjusted their relationship to accommodate the gayness. They maintained their marriage and life together as parents, even though it was not a conventional lifestyle. However, other couples shifted to the next stage.

ANTICIPATING THE FUTURE

This stage illustrates the continuous uncertainty experienced by both partners in their adjustment to the husband's sexuality. Some wives were uncertain whether they were willing to renegotiate their relationships and accommodate their husbands' sexuality. Barbara, who had been married to Peter for eight years and had two young children, attempted to accommodate to the situation but adjusted by opting for a trial separation. Barbara and Peter were unsure whether they wished legally to end their marriage. They were still committed to each other and the maintenance of their family life and had not ruled out the possibility of a reconciliation. Illustrating his uncertainty about the future, Peter said:

> I don't see that the marriage is over. I can quite envisage in the future, say ten – fifteen years, whatever, maybe only two years, that we can get back together again. . . . I don't know what I can do about my sexuality, whether that will ever change again or whether I'll ever be able to revert back to being able to cope in a heterosexual environment. I don't know. I think we had a good marriage and I think we had sufficient between us to make a marriage work. . . . She's only twenty-eight and I felt she needed a free hand to run her

own life again. I think to a certain extent she has that within the limitations of money and the kids. In some ways I hope she doesn't find anyone else in the hope that when we both feel ready we might reunite.

Barbara also joined the same self-help group as Christine, but in contrast to Christine she decided that she could not accommodate her husband's gayness. She explained:

I had come to the realisation that the women who had been living with it for several years were going through exactly the same emotions as I was having just found out. I decided that I didn't want to be going through the same emotions in ten to fifteen years' time because they weren't very nice. Initially I felt that I could handle it, then I came to the realisation that nothing was going to change and I thought that I was worth more and that I was destined for better things. I took a lot of emotional battering before I decided that it was the end. . . . I know that I saw it through to the end.

Jeremy and Carla, who had been married for thirteen years, stayed together for six months after the disclosure of his sexuality. They sought professional help and went to a marriage guidance counsellor several times. However, reflecting on the strategies she employed at this stage, Carla said:

I thought, 'Can one live with this?' I was thinking about the children and everything, as one does. I was becoming crosser and crosser. . . . I suggested a compromise, one night out a week, no questions asked and the rest of the time you devote more time to the family. It wasn't just in terms of going out with other men but the whole impetus, all his energy was elsewhere. He was getting politically involved and it was just going through his whole life. The whole thing seemed to be so anti-family. He said that he couldn't form a relationship if I only allowed him out one night a week . . . so I said that in that case you had better go.

Jeremy did not want a divorce and expressed his opposition to splitting up:

The thought of divorce was an anathema to me and it would be the one thing that upset me when we had a row that Carla would say perhaps we ought to get a divorce. . . . I spent about two years dithering, not knowing quite what to do. Feeling that things can't go on. . . . I couldn't face getting a divorce and telling Carla that I thought it was all over and couldn't face what would happen about the children.

Their husbands' sexuality was not the only issue that concerned most of the wives. For many it was coming to terms with the disclosure that their husbands were emotionally involved with someone else and that infidelity had occurred. Carla said that she could not accept Jeremy's infidelity. Although she acknowledged that not all marriages were monogamous, she did not feel that she could accept this type of behaviour in her marriage. As she explained:

> I sometimes wonder if I could have come to terms with it, but I don't think I could. I think it's probably difficult for most people to stay faithful, completely, in a marriage. I don't think infidelity matters, I think it's good to be discreet about it. But I think that if the future of your marriage has to have infidelity on somebody's part built into it, then, for me, that rather knocks the stuffing out of it. . . . The odd fling or discreet romance, fine, but I think if it is there all the time it's different. We all have a choice in life and you can't have everything you want.

As Carla said, she felt that we all have a choice, and she and Barbara chose to end their marriages. Consequently they shifted to the next stage in this process and became lone parents.

COPING ALONE

Becoming a lone parent does not necessarily mean a total separation from the financial, emotional or practical support of the ex-partner (Bohannan, 1970; Hart, 1976; Smart, 1984; Vaughan, 1986), yet many people do live in isolation after being separated from a couple-centred social life (Elliot, 1986; Hardey, 1989). Although living apart, the couples in my research were still in constant interaction with each other. The men contributed financially and practically. However, the women's roles became more complex. They still had the major responsibility for the children, were in paid employment and continued to support the men in an affective role by listening to their problems and nursing them when they were ill. For these women, 'coping alone' did not lead to relinquishing their caring role as wives and mothers.

Carla divorced Jeremy for unreasonable behaviour and they had joint custody of their two children, aged twelve and ten. Carla and Jeremy still maintained close contact, both as committed friends and as parents. They lived near each other and met periodically. As Jeremy described the situation:

> We all went with friends to the seaside in the summer, that worked well. We have joint custody of the children. . . . We still talk to each other and we went to the parents' evening at the school. The children like to see us together. Annie told her next-door neighbour, 'They're quite fond of each other, you know.'

As Jeremy said in the previous stage, he had been concerned about the effects of a divorce on his children. However, after the divorce he neutralised his fears:

> I think the children have got over it quite well. They've had their traumas but they don't seem particularly upset or worried about coming round here. Annie is always very affectionate when she leaves and they only live around the corner. Apart from the trauma of my leaving, they haven't had to change houses or anything like that.

In the process of adjusting to being a divorced father, Jeremy was planning to find a home where his children could spend more time with him, as he explained:

> I'm looking for a base. I've been here for a year in this house. . . . I'm looking for somewhere where the children can come and stay with me. I do miss the children. I notice occasionally I miss them more than other times. In a way I'd like to see them more often.

Although Carla and Jeremy had joint custody, their children lived with her. She had worked as a part-time teacher during the marriage, and since the divorce she had secured a full-time teaching post. Carla described her experiences of being a divorced lone mother in a society which values two-parent families but devalues lone parenting:

> It would be nice to have a constant companion, you know, to talk to in the evenings and all the rest of it. I suppose when you are freshly divorced you miss having a man around and as a father figure for the children as well. I suppose because our society is still nurtured

on the idea of the two-parent family. . . . As far as they are concerned we have split up because we don't get on. . . . Things seem to have worked out quite well really. They see him once or twice a week. He cooks them a meal and they watch TV and talk. I'm sure once he gets a place of his own they will go round there more often. But living in a rented place there isn't much space or privacy. . . . He still loves his children and they love him and I hope that because of that they will come out unscathed from this and will just see it as a parental upset. They certainly seem fine.

Carla's life had changed considerably since she and Jeremy divorced. She discussed both the fresh opportunities of being an independent woman and at the same time the constraints of living alone. As she explained:

It's a strange feeling knowing you take all the decisions yourself. It has its nice side, though. You don't have to say is it all right to have so and so around or can we go somewhere?. . . But it's quite shattering really when you have been used to doing things together. . . . At weekends I still see the same friends but it is a threesome instead of foursome. . . . Jeremy always used to sort out the bills but now I have to do it myself.

Like Carla, Jeremy was a full-time teacher, although his lifestyle, unlike Carla's, was not restricted by the responsibility of caring for the children. He acknowledged this: 'I do realise I have greater freedom in that I don't have to worry about babysitters and that Carla has quite a hard time in working full-time and looking after them.'

For some years Jeremy and Carla maintained a good relationship and were constantly adjusting to living apart and being alone. Neither of them formed a new permanent relationship. Sadly, Jeremy became terminally ill and Carla and the children visited him frequently. At times Carla played the role of carer by helping to nurse him. Not long before he died, they remarried.

Another couple who had shifted through all four stages were Barbara and Peter. In the previous stage, Barbara was uncertain whether she could cope and adjust to Peter's shift in sexual identity. She eventually opted for a trial separation. Unlike Jeremy, Peter lived some distance away from his marital home, but he also maintained close contact with his wife and children.

Although he did not live in the same household, Peter was concerned about his children and maintained his commitment to them. He continued to help support them financially and regularly spent time with them. As he said:

> I love my children enormously. I do find them difficult to cope with, a couple of days at weekends is enough. . . . I'd like to think that in the future I could have them for holidays. . . . I think it important that they feel that Barbara and I still have a marriage. Maybe not in the conventional sense but we are still extremely close. We have two or three days together and that's fine but then we find the little things that used to niggle us start again. So two or three days together is enough so we get the best of both worlds. They don't seem to have suffered from the situation. I desperately want to stay close to the children. I would hate to think that if one of them is gay that they would go through the traumas I went through trying to discover myself. And I'd like to feel that I was at hand in case they need someone to talk to.

In this stage of 'coping alone', Barbara joined a group for lone parents. However, in interaction with other members she rejected their adjustments to the identity of a lone parent and defined herself as more confident than them. As she said:

> I go to Gingerbread, I see there a bitterness but I'm not aware of any bitterness on my part. He's left me free to lead my own life and he's leading his. I had a call from a woman and she'd been alone for four years. I felt that she was still waiting for him to come back. Women don't see their own value. I was a confident teenager but over the past eight years my confidence went down. But I have got over that now.

As noted above, most wives experience a lack of self-esteem on the disclosure of their husband's gayness, and Barbara did lose much of her former confidence. However, since making the decision to separate from her husband she had gradually become more confident, increased her self-esteem, had a job that she enjoyed and was in the process of becoming more independent of her husband. Nevertheless she was still very fond of Peter and described their continuous contact and his apparent dependence on her:

> I put more pressures on myself in not wanting him to do anything in the house and garden when he comes at the weekends. I feel very much now that what he wants from me is a 'mum'. If he has any problems he phones me even now. He wants a 'mum' and from

what I've heard from others it's the same. At the moment life is quite easy in that I have someone to look after the children, I've got a full-time job which I enjoy tremendously.

Gradually, Barbara had shifted through the four stages of this process of 'becoming a lone parent', yet in this final stage of 'coping alone' there were still times when she wondered if she had made the right decision to separate from Peter. As she said:

Occasionally I get times when I think I would like him back, but it's always times when he's not around. As soon as I see him I know it wouldn't work. The wishing is for what might have been. Those times are becoming further apart.

Barbara was enjoying her new-found independence, but she was saddened by the negative implications of her new identity and the lifestyle of her children. However, employing a neutralising strategy, Barbara emphasised Peter's positive qualities and the roles he still performed as a husband and father:

There is something I find hard. That's watching the kids miss their dad. He comes once a fortnight because I work every other weekend. He comes for the weekend to look after them. I think he's been tremendous actually. When I look at other husbands I think I'm very fortunate in that he does think the world of his kids and he still thinks a lot of me, I know. He supports us financially. . . . He cuts the grass. I don't think that there is anything he did I can't do on my own now. I know if there is anything I can't do he will do it for me.

Barbara had said that she had been quite happy in the first stage of getting married and having children and had not expected to get divorced, assuming that she would be married to Peter for ever. As she shifted through the second and third stages in the process of becoming a lone parent, however, she had been very unhappy and lost much of her self-esteem. Yet in the fourth stage she expressed a positive identity of being a lone parent. As she said:

At the moment I am quite happy on my own and don't feel the need to have anyone to share my life. . . . I feel happy about myself now. I feel stronger now than I was while we were together in that I used to let his opinions matter very much to me. . . . It was important that he was happy. I'm now more assertive. The only thing I would change is my weight. I think I'm quite capable. There isn't much I couldn't do now if I put my mind to it.

Peter and Barbara were living apart, but they maintained a relatively satisfactory relationship together. They were fond of, and supported, each other. Both were actively involved in the care of their children.

CONCLUSION

This study has attempted to shed some light on the experiences of a group of parents who generally lead hidden lives. It has illustrated that for some women who discovered that the father of their children was gay, becoming a lone parent was not a single event but a gradual process of shifting, back and forth, through four overlapping stages.

In the first stage, 'getting married and having children', the couples met, married and had children. They expected to live conventional lifestyles. However, marriage and children did not constitute a validation of the fathers' heterosexuality, for in the second stage the husbands disclosed their gayness. In this stage of 'keeping the family together', contrary to common-sense predictions, the parents did not immediately separate and divorce. Instead, many adjusted to the gayness and renegotiated their marriage contract. Some maintained a two-parent family, albeit one based on an alternative lifestyle. Others shifted to the third stage, 'anticipating the future', when they assessed their situation and deliberated on what the future held. Some might shift back to the previous stage, others to the next. This fourth stage was 'coping alone', when the women decided to separate from or divorce their gay husbands. Although they no longer lived together, both parents remained in contact, giving and receiving emotional, financial and practical support. Nevertheless, the women were constrained by having the major responsibility for their children and running the home, and at the same time they were coping with full-time employment. This was in contrast to their partners, who were also adjusting to coping alone but had the opportunity to pursue their gay lifestyles. On the other hand the women, who often expressed their uncertainty and misgivings about their decision to end their marriages and become lone parents, slowly grew more confident and in some areas of their lives enjoyed a new-found independence. Clearly, becoming a lone parent is a gradual process.

Following these parents through this process has also revealed that, contrary to popular assumptions, heterosexual marriage and parenthood are not a validation of heterosexuality. What is also illuminating from their accounts is their resistance to defining themselves or their lifestyles as deviant, for they constantly employed various neutralisation techniques and strategies to deny that their lifestyles were abnormal. This was clear from the positive aspects they emphasised in opposition to societal reaction to sexual deviations and lone parents. Like Voysey's (1975) study of parents of handicapped children and Burgoyne and Clark's (1984) research on step-families, they presented their lifestyles as not unlike their images of 'normal' families and parents. For whether these people maintained two-parent families by creating alternative lifestyles or became lone parents, they resisted defining themselves as socially deviant. Consequently, this study has revealed not only a gradual process in which some women married to gays became lone parents but also their perceptions of how marriage and parenthood should be. These are reflections and echoes of moral, political and social expectations surrounding marriage and parenthood which may prove difficult to live up to.

8 The conflicting experiences of lone parenthood

Sandra Shaw

The title of this chapter reflects the fact that the experience of lone parenthood is full of contradictions. Often the negative aspects are stressed – specifically loneliness and lack of money. However, there are also positive aspects of lone parenthood, which will be referred to in order to give a more rounded view of women's experience of lone parenthood and their attitudes towards remarriage. In addition, it should become clear that individuals and their lives are very complicated, resulting in contradictory responses, so that, for example, being alone can be seen by the same person as having both negative and positive aspects. It is also true that our views and expectations change in the light of experiences which are continually occurring; in this respect those women referred to here will continue to change and develop their ideas.

The views expressed in this chapter have arisen out of the responses given by separated or divorced women, interviewed about their experiences as lone parents. All those referred to have had their names changed in order to maintain confidentiality. The women interviewed had been lone parents for around two years or more at the time of the interview. Some women had spent a long period as lone parents – four, six, eight and even twelve years – and had thus had considerable time to reflect on their experience of marriage, the ending of a marriage, and lone parenthood. The ages of those interviewed ranged from late twenties to early forties, with one, two or three children actually at home, ranging in age from twenty-one months to seventeen years. The majority of those interviewed were either totally or partially dependent on Income Support, and therefore living on a low income.

Contacting those interviewed was done primarily through the network of support groups for lone parents that exists in

Sheffield, and in total, twenty-five women were contacted. In addition to interviewing, I also attended the meetings of one of these groups for three months, both participating and observing, thus adding another source of information to the research. The basic orientation of the research is woman-centred, by which I mean that I have been concerned throughout the fieldwork, analysis of material and writing-up to allow the respondents' own views to be represented, and to contribute to the development of any insights into the experience of lone parenthood for women. All those interviewed were asked about their past marriage or marriages, their experiences as a lone parent, and their hopes for the future, as inevitably we are all to some extent shaped by our pasts, and perceive our futures from where we are in the present.

Whilst each individual's personal history may be unique, it is still possible to make some generalisations based on a continuity of responses between women. Women were asked what they thought were the worst and the best things about being a lone parent, and the first part of this chapter reflects responses made in relation to the former. It then goes on to consider what are seen to be the best things about being a lone parent.

NEGATIVE EXPERIENCES OF LONE PARENTHOOD

When asked what was the worst thing about being a lone parent, women invariably responded, in some form, with references to the financial situation and to loneliness. The former is dealt with only briefly in this chapter, not least because it has been dealt with well elsewhere (Ashley, 1983; DHSS, 1974; Graham, 1987a; Marsden, 1973; Millar, 1987, 1988, 1989); the latter is considered at greater length. Concerning finance, what is clearly implied in the women's responses is a lack of money, or having insufficient money to be able to live without constantly worrying about paying the bills, feeding the children, and similar practical tasks. Money, or the lack of it, becomes an obsession, as one respondent stated: 'I think that probably one of the main things is that it seems all money-orientated this, and it shouldn't be.' Lack of money also contributes to loneliness, in the sense that a woman's social life may be limited owing to a lack of resources (Green and Hebron, 1988).

It is possible for anyone to be lonely at some time in their life, and as another respondent put it, 'You can have people round you all day long and all night, but you're still alone.' When the women interviewed talk about loneliness, they are speaking of something very specific. Loneliness means lack of an adult companion to talk to, to hold, to be with, who loves them, understands them, and puts them first, before anything else. What these women are referring to is the fact that they do not have a partner. They are partnerless, in a society which finds it easier to deal with couples (Elliot, 1986).

The fact that these women feel a need for 'someone special' does not mean that they are more unhappy than other individuals in society who experience the same feelings. Neither does it mean that they are permanently depressed, or negative about their lives. On the contrary, they are for the most part extremely positive about themselves, and optimistic about their futures.

In this respect, most of the women interviewed attended lone-parent support groups, which provided a social outlet for both parents and children, as well as practical and emotional support. Other women interviewed also had alternative social outlets. Family played a very important part in the lives of some women and their children, again providing practical, emotional and even financial support to some. Finally, friends were very important – particularly women friends. Friendship was portrayed as something much more significant to these women after their marriage had ended than it had been during it, and was very highly valued (Allan, 1989).

Whether or not to remarry was also not the only issue considered when we discussed the future. Trying to arrive at an answer to this question does not fill women's lives; therefore this chapter is considering only one aspect of what a woman's future might or might not hold. Many women were actively progressing towards returning to work and supporting themselves, by retraining or various types of education, and were generally positive about their potential futures as lone parents. However, the question of remarriage is an important one, as it reflects social pressures about unmarried adults, particularly those past a certain age (Allen, 1987; Collins, this volume, pp. 156–75), and also social concerns about lone-parent households, and whether or not children can be brought up effectively in such a family unit.

Financial difficulties and loneliness are frequently and

consistently expressed negative aspects of being a lone parent. These problems raise the question of whether or not remarriage is considered an attractive possibility for the future, by women themselves. Bradshaw (1989) writes that there is a public interest in encouraging women to remarry, as it would save the state money. He also argues that there would be benefits for both parents and children in the 'reconstitution' of the family. Whilst financial matters may not be paramount when it comes to making a decision to remarry, he suggests that there are financial measures which might encourage this decision. He ends by suggesting that this might include a grant as a 'lump sum reconstitution grant as a kind of dowry' (1989, p. 25).

Yet lone-parent families are families in their own right, and do not need reconstituting like a packet of mashed potatoes by adding the missing ingredient – in this case a man. It is important that the views of those concerned should be heard and taken note of by those in a position to influence policy-making. Actively encouraging remarriage also seems a dubious policy option when it is generally accepted that second marriages are even more likely to end in divorce than first marriages, and 'despite popular beliefs remarriage does not seem to solve the problems generated by divorce at either a personal or public level' (Burgoyne *et al.*, 1987, p. 39).

It should not be assumed that all divorced women desperately want to remarry, and that the only reason they do not is because they are too old, too fat, or too unattractive, and cannot find anyone who will take them on. Generally, statistics on rates of remarriage are taken to indicate that a woman's chances of remarriage decline rapidly as she ages, particularly after the age of thirty-four – unlike men's (Haskey, this volume, pp. 19–46). This interpretation tends to be taken for granted, without questioning whether or not these women want to remarry.

Throughout the interviews women were allowed to express their ideas about their hopes for the future, and about remarriage as an option. Respondents never suggested that they might be too old, too unattractive, or would not be able to find anyone. They never presented themselves as rejects on the marriage market. Most women do in fact have mixed views about remarriage, which are affected by their own experiences of marriage and lone parenthood. It is here that the many positive results of being a lone parent need to be considered, as these have a direct bearing on how women feel about remarriage.

POSITIVE EXPERIENCES OF LONE PARENTHOOD

All respondents expressed positive feelings about being a lone parent, arising out of gains they felt they had made, thus giving further confirmation of Sharpe's finding that divorced mothers may be 'happier alone' (1984, p. 205). Their gains are hard-won and would not be given up lightly. The benefits of being alone may be fundamental, or may at first glance appear trivial. Some of the most fundamental gains may be identified as emotional, and these can be seen to revolve around ideas of independence, pride and self-esteem, confidence, and a feeling of doing a hard job (that is, parenting) well. Wendy, aged forty, who had experienced a very traumatic time in her four years as a lone parent – including problems with her two eldest children and having recently been evicted from the marital home – still felt able to say: 'I like my independence. I wouldn't like to go back. It's hard. I think you take a lot of knocks, and some of them take a hell of a lot of getting over, and you think you're not gonna get over them but somehow you do.' Barbara, at thirty-six and with only one child, had been a lone parent for the same length of time and had a very positive approach to life in general. She expressed herself both forcefully and at times eloquently, as when she stated: 'I think it's just a sense of achievement, you know. I mean you feel like a phoenix rising from the ashes – your marriage being in ashes – to suddenly rise again.'

Jane, thirty-one, a lone parent since before the birth of the younger of her two children, who at this point was only twenty-one months old, was one of those interviewed who was not attending a support group for lone parents. She had instead developed her own social network via the local church she attended and was very determined not to 'let this divorce break me up, which it could have done. In fact, if anything, it's made me a lot stronger, because I was determined that I wasn't going to give in to it.'

Finally, thirty-two-year-old Rachel, mentioned below as having problems accepting her new status of lone parent, expressed this sense of achievement, also felt by others: 'At the end of it all you can turn round and think, "I've brought those children up, or child up, on my own", and you can look and you think, "Well, I've done it".'

Throughout the interviews women consistently made statements referring to these emotional gains, which clearly counteract the more negative feelings and experiences associated with lone parenthood. Such gains, arising as they do out of difficult times, are very highly valued and reflect a sense of pride and achievement.

In addition to the major emotional gains that respondents spoke of as coming from their experiences of lone parenthood, it is also often said that it is the little things in life that can make or break a marriage. In the same way, it can be the little things that deter a woman from remarriage. These include having to wash someone's dirty socks, having to iron shirts, and being expected to cook meals to order. As Jane stated: 'I don't have to worry about meals. We can have what we want. I don't have to wash and iron shirts and trousers. Oh, it's heaven!' Although these might appear to be 'little things', taken together they represent a stereotypical view of traditional marriage, with women seeing to men's needs. This is the type of marriage that most of these women have experienced, even in the so-called 'liberated' 1980s, and these small gains are significant. What is interesting, however, is that when women do visualise what a future marriage might involve, some seem to expect to fulfil these duties once again. It is therefore not clear to what extent they are questioning traditional roles for men and women. In addition, the following gains, whilst perhaps being small in themselves, do represent something much more fundamental for women – namely, the achievement of being in control. They include being able to go out alone without permission, not having to ask for money and not having to consult a man before spending money.

With regard to financial matters, women were not always without control over money during their marriage. Their experiences of the economic aspects of marriage were very diverse. Some women, even after giving up paid work, had total responsibility for the financial management of the household, even to the extent of holding the chequebook, or in one case being handed the pay packet. Nevertheless, women as mothers, not making a financial contribution to the household, still tended to see income as the husband's, and to feel obliged to ask permission to spend money – particularly on themselves.

From the point of view of coping financially as a lone parent, many women have significant experience of managing resources during marriage (Pahl, 1989), although of course, after separation or divorce they are most likely to be living on a reduced income. It is significant, however, that even women who appeared to have quite a lot of control over money during marriage still referred to the benefits of controlling the household finances themselves. The important thing is that they no longer have to consult someone else, or seek permission before spending money or allocating resources.

A fourth issue was that of being alone, and relates to the benefits of not having a permanent and full-time partner. As has already been indicated, not having a partner is seen in our society as a lack, but there are also benefits to being alone. Once again, this illustrates the contradictory nature of being a lone parent. The advantages of being alone include being able to watch what you want to on television, going to bed to sleep, not waking up every morning with someone's head on the pillow next to you, and not having someone there all the time, under your feet.

Women's attitudes towards lone parenthood as opposed to remarriage are clearly affected by their previous experience of marriage and by the breakdown of a marriage. Three issues in particular featured time and again during the interview in discussions of the possibility of remarriage: wariness, reluctance or inability to trust, and fear of getting hurt again. Adultery was often mentioned, either as the cause of the breakdown of the marriage or as a contributory factor, although of course individual circumstances vary (Lawson, 1989). Several husbands had been having an extra-marital relationship before the final separation, and left their wives in order to live with someone else. Some women seemed prepared to tolerate (or perhaps put up with) affairs because they loved their husbands, but when an affair was too close to home – that is, with a neighbour or with the wife's best friend – enough was enough.

From the point of view of the partner who has been left, the most traumatic scenario seems to be when she was not aware that an affair had been going on, and in fact felt that the marriage was good. This highlights the fact that in every marriage there are two marriages, and each partner has their own perception of what is occurring, and whether or not the relationship is satisfactory (Bernard, 1973). In these circumstances, being left is devastating and it can take months, or in some cases years, to come to terms with the end of the marriage.

Rachel, for example, was only just getting her life back together again at the time of the interview, after eight years as a lone parent. She had spent the first six years of that time not acknowledging the fact that she was a lone parent, appearing to conceive of herself as still being in some kind of marriage. This in itself would clearly affect whether or not a person would consider remarriage. She stated: 'It's only two years, probably a bit longer, since I stopped wearing my wedding ring.' Her husband initially had regular (daily) contact with their child, and he even had his own key to the house eight years on. She also lent him money from her state benefit, even though he worked and was living with a woman who also worked. 'I still thought, while ever he's there – so in one respect, I was married, and in another respect, no I wasn't because I had to manage on my own.' It took several years before she asked herself, 'Time was passing by and where was I?'

Whatever the circumstances, women express most anger and hurt about the fact that they have been betrayed and deceived. It is these feelings which lead them to be wary of another marriage, and contribute to their inability to trust. Generally, women feel sad about this, but unable totally to control or conquer this lack of trust. So, for example, Barbara, whose husband left her to live with someone else, states:

> The thing that I think I resent most about being a single parent is the loss of faith in people, because I think everyone you meet, especially men, you're looking for an ulterior motive, and it's not fair really, because not all men are the same, like not all women are the same. I trust the chap I'm with at the moment ninety-nine per cent. It's the other one per cent, and likewise I don't think I can ever give myself a hundred per cent to any man again, because I did to my first husband and he betrayed my trust.

The complexities of lone parenthood are such that many of the gains of being a lone parent have a negative aspect. The things mentioned as possible reasons for remarriage have also featured in alternative format as reasons for not remarrying. Prominent among reasons given for considering remarriage are being alone, being lonely, needing someone to discuss things with, wanting someone else to make decisions sometimes, just for you, and even someone to laugh with. All of these are seen as attractive reasons for remarriage, and as Jane said, 'I would love the closeness and the intimacy and all the little personal things that make up a marriage.' Although the need for physical contact was mentioned by many women this does not necessarily imply sexual contact, as women most commonly express the desire to be touched, to hold hands, to be held and to be cuddled by a man.

The romantic ideal also features in women's responses. This might relate to the ritual of courtship and marriage, for example through the romance of a wedding and the romance of love. Although Rachel had clearly been deeply hurt by the end of her marriage, she might consider remarrying if she could 'have a big sticky-out red frock. Like Scarlett O'Hara!' Jackie, twenty-nine, also referred to her longing to wear a beautiful white dress and experience the 'proper' wedding she missed out on first time round – although she was quite cynical about what would happen afterwards. In addition, some women have an idealised notion of a perfect relationship, which can be achieved, even in the light of past negative experiences. In other words, they are eternally optimistic.

We also have to bear in mind the social pressures which might exist on women to remarry. These can originate with government policy, or with individuals or groups giving advice to policy-makers. At a more immediate level for the lone parent, the views of family and friends might be expected to have some impact, as will the particular image which is conjured up by the label 'lone parent'.

CHANGE OVER TIME

Some previous studies on divorce and lone parenthood will now be considered to see whether or not there is any evidence of change in social attitudes towards lone parents and, in particular, in women's views on lone parenthood and remarriage. Goode's

Women in Divorce (1965) refers to a study of divorced women carried out in Detroit in 1948. Goode's thesis is that the status of divorce is so problematic that divorced women will quickly be 'reassimilated to the status of "married"' (1965, p. 204). A divorced mother was of lower social status than a married or widowed mother, and there were therefore pressures towards remarriage as a solution of the 'institutional ambiguity' of the status 'divorcee mother' (1965, p. 210).

Many of the pressures Goode refers to can be placed together under the heading of social pressures, and would include criticism and advice, living in a 'couple society' and not fitting in as an older unmarried person, and being seen as a potential threat to spouses – and, of course, the perceived need for children to have two parents. These pressures would generally originate with family and kin.

In addition, Goode suggests that there was the inconvenience of not having a permanent sexual partner, which posed particular difficulties for women: 'in our society the woman in particular is conditioned to respond less fully and adequately in a sexual relationship if it is defined as purely for sexual pleasure' (1965, p. 214). There was in effect little room for adult non-marrieds in American society at the time, and 'almost all roads for the divorcee [would] lead to remarriage' (*ibid.*). Remarriage would furnish the solution, as it would provide the divorcee with a status and a prescribed role with which she and others would feel comfortable. A period of lone parenthood thus became a period of adjustment, where the divorcee moved from becoming a divorced person to becoming 'a potential spouse' (1965, p. 125).

Marsden, in *Mothers Alone* (1973), based on a survey of unsupported mothers (of different types) on National Assistance (forerunner of Income Support) carried out in 1965 and 1966, considers whether or not remarriage (or marriage) might be a solution to the problems of lone parenthood. He concludes that there might be pressures both for and against remarriage, stating that only about a quarter of respondents actually wanted to remarry, a quarter would consider it, and the remainder did not want to. However, he suggests rather ambiguously at this point in his discussion that a woman's chances of remarrying – that is, her eligibility – might affect her response, thereby seeming to cast doubt on the veracity of women's responses (1973, pp. 157–9).

Hart, in *When Marriage Ends* (1976), presents a study of a club for the divorced and separated, which includes both men and women. She paints a very negative picture of what it means to be separated or divorced and suggests that remarriage is the solution which will be sought by most individuals. Again, this relates to the status of the unmarried, who are held in contempt, or pitied, or perhaps resented (1976, p. 37). However, she repeats the claim – made by Goode and implied by Marsden – that the prospects of remarriage decline, particularly for women, as the age of thirty approaches. She also states that most (73 per cent) of her respondents wanted to remarry, and that particular handicaps were age, money, lack of access (to potential partners) and parenthood. Again, it is taken as given that women are less well favoured, and the pressure to remarry is seen as largely a social one, due to the ambivalent status of the divorcee and the fact that we live in a 'couple society'.

For Hart, 'Divorce is a process of endless becoming, hopefully becoming something else' (1976, p. 221) – that is, married. Few divorcees become reconciled to remaining unmarried. Hart finishes by stating: 'As long as divorce remains a minority problem in Britain and social life continues to be organised so consistently around the married couple, such a solution to the divorcee's difficulties is bound to be widely sought' (1976, p. 230).

So – does the situation remain the same, and do the same social pressures still exist for divorced and separated women to remarry? Or, even if such pressures do exist, do women today react to them differently? One more recent study in the United States, by Arendell, *Mothers and Divorce* (1986), indicates that a change in attitudes has taken place since Goode conducted his survey. Arendell uses the word 'ambivalence' to describe women's feelings towards remarriage:

Some stated strongly that they would never marry again, but the majority said they were uncertain or doubtful about it, and some had already declined marriage proposals. Their ambivalence about remarriage seemed rooted in a new feeling of independence, a new sense of self that required protection: their hard-won gains might be lost in a new marriage (1986, p. 142).

When considering remarriage, women weigh up the costs and

benefits, and remarriage may diminish in attractiveness. For most women, remarriage would involve sacrifices.

This section has attempted to show that there has been a change in the social climate, that it has become more acceptable for women to bring up children alone, and that women are not subjected to the same kind of pressure to remarry as previously. This evidence should, however, be treated with caution. Phillips's history of divorce in Western society, *Putting Asunder* (1988), notes that 'We should not look for a simple linear evolution of attitudes toward divorce in a positive direction, however, for shifts in opinion [have] varied according to specific social and political context as well as according to class and gender' (1988, p. 636). In other words, changes in attitudes do not necessarily progress in a positive manner, and in this respect the present political context may be contributing to a regressive change of attitudes towards lone parenthood.

CONCLUSION

The responses given in this research would certainly bear out what Arendell states: that lone parenthood has positive results for women, and remarriage is seen as something which would involve sacrifices. Ambivalence is, however, a vague term, and I would suggest that some women have much stronger attitudes about the choice between remarriage and staying a lone parent. Some would certainly like to remarry, and this represents their hope for the future. Others, however, definitely do not see remarriage as part of their future.

It might therefore be appropriate to think of women's views as arranged along a continuum, but to bear in mind, as indicated at the beginning of this chapter, that these views may change. At one extreme are those who wish to remarry, whatever their previous experience of marriage; at the other are those who do not want to remarry. In between these two extremes women express a range of opinions, which reflect the contradictory nature of their feelings on the matter. It should be stressed, however, that even women who express a definite desire to remarry qualify what they say, and anticipate that a new marriage will not be like their old one.

In addition, several women also state that they would rather live with someone than get married again – cohabitation clearly being seen as something qualitatively different to marriage. Finally, there are those with their own unique attitude towards marriage, as evidenced by Theresa who, at the age of thirty, had already been married three times – divorced, widowed and separated. She would still try marriage again, even though it had never proved entirely satisfactory for her. She was very philosophical about this, concluding that 'marriage is to me what cucumber is to some other people. I like it, but it doesn't agree with me!' There seems little evidence of family and friends exerting the kind of pressure to remarry that might have been experienced by earlier generations of lone parents, although of course they may wish to see someone happily remarried. Most women do maintain that there is still stigma attached to the label 'lone parent', but this is not enough in itself to persuade them that the benefits of remarrying will inevitably outweigh the costs.

Over time, women who are lone parents do make fundamental gains, arising out of their everyday experiences. Whilst achieving such gains, they are actively engaged in renegotiating their status in society as lone parents, and in the process challenging the negative stereotypes associated with lone parenthood. In the long term this can only be beneficial for the women themselves and the children they care for.

9 The transition from lone-parent family to step-family

Stephen Collins

This chapter is about lone-parent families at the time when the parent marries or remarries. Based on the experiences of some lone parents who were members of a group for mutual support, it explores some of the factors affecting their decision to set up a home with another adult, and identifies some of the emotional and practical issues involved. I shall argue that the decision and its consequences bring together pressures of two distinct but inextricably involved kinds: those of a private, personal nature and those relating to wider social processes.

First there are the pressures of a personal kind which come from the particular circumstances of someone's life. These will include the personalities of the people involved, their practical and material situation, their feelings and beliefs, and the opportunities and luck that come their way. Such a list means that each individual's experience is unique, and bears out what has been apparent throughout this book – that lone parents are such a diverse group that it is well-nigh meaningless to think in terms of a 'typical' lone parent. Diversity, though, is a human characteristic, and so long as we take due account of it, and do not try to reduce people's experience to oversimplified general assertions, it is possible to identify things about them in given circumstances that are frequently true or usually the case. Though there will always be an abundance of exceptions, we can still talk approximate sense provided we do not ignore these exceptions or try to twist them into conforming with general rules.

People's lives, though, cannot be understood in purely private terms, for they are played out against the background of a society which embodies values and opinions (Richards and Light, 1986). Social attitudes to marriage have a profound influence on individual lives and represent a comment on them. As well, therefore, as the circumstances of an individual's life, we have to try to understand the ideological pressures that bear down on that life. Ideology is notoriously hard to explain (Boudon, 1988; Todd, 1988) and is not therefore always a helpful term, but here I use the word to mean the ideas and beliefs that form the taken-for-granted and widely held notions of the nature of life, of how things are and of how they ought to be. For all their common-sense quality, these ideas and beliefs are not objective 'truth', but express and sustain the wishes and requirements of dominant groups in society – dominant numerically as well as in terms of economic and moral power.

I shall not attempt any detailed explanation of the ideologies that affect the lives of lone parents, for explaining them is a supplementary question to the way in which these lives are influenced by the ideological climate in which they occur. It will become clear, however, that I believe these ideologies do not have any necessary authority, and can legitimately be disregarded or repudiated by men and women of goodwill. Parents especially may need to be critical in their consideration of these ideologies if they are to understand and control them, and if they are to protect their children from beliefs and assumptions that are not appropriate to their particular circumstances. It seems to me to be in the nature of ideology that it slips imperceptibly from being a description of how things are to becoming an assertion that this is how things should be. The fact that most people do something does not mean that it is right for everyone to do it, though, and parents pondering what best to do in their individual lives may judge it wiser to ignore the beckonings of ideologies and choose an individual solution. The success of many non-traditional families (Lamb, 1982; Macklin, 1980) shows that the majority domestic arrangement does not suit every case.

INDUCEMENTS TO MARRIAGE

The interplay between individual lives and the dominant ideology against which they are enacted is illustrated by the decision of lone parents to marry or remarry, and has to be understood if we are to make sense of that decision. (Throughout this chapter I shall use the term 'marriage' to describe the establishment of a permanent domestic relationship with another adult. It is not important to the argument whether a civil or religious ceremony is involved, or whether the arrangement is an unofficial one – though it may, of course, be important to the protagonists – and this definition of marriage could include homosexual relationships.)

Many lone parents have had experiences of marriage that might be expected to discourage them from repeating the experiment, but despite this, remarriage is common among lone parents (Haskey, 1983). Two factors insistently draw people into marriage or remarriage, often despite earlier experiences. The first of these is the frequently cheerless life of many lone parents. Among the lone parents on whose experiences this chapter is based, there was a predominantly dispirited mood which was often perilously close to disabling depression. Part of the reason for this was the pain of rejection or disappointment that came from a broken relationship, but a common and more tangible cause was economic. Many lone parents are impoverished (Millar, 1989); this, as well as the obvious drawbacks in terms of securing a comfortable standard of living, has a more subtle consequence for morale. Western industrial societies articulate their values in material ways, and dignified poverty is pretty well impossible in such a context. For many lone parents, their poverty is as much a source of embarrassment as a practical inconvenience, for it convicts them in their own eyes of failure, and symbolically expresses the idea that society is less impressed with their efforts to keep a home for their children than contemptuous of their struggles and achievements.

In consequence, many lone parents feel undervalued, and experience a recurring sense of failure when at a loss to explain to children why they cannot provide the clothes, the holidays or the school trips that have passed from the realm of luxury to that of normal expectation for the majority of the population (Richards, 1989). In such a position, marriage may seem to offer a way out. This is sometimes an illusion, though, for although it is probably true that remarriage improves the financial circumstances of most lone parents (Maclean and Eekelaar, 1983; Zick and Smith, 1988) there are cases in which it does just the opposite, as in the case of widows who lose their pension on remarriage. Moreover, the long-term economic consequences of remarriage are not easy to calculate, especially when the new partner is unemployed and likely to remain so, for changes in social security regulations may well wipe out any short-term benefit. Obviously, an unemployed lone parent is likely to be substantially better off by marrying someone in full-time work, but in practice the financial profit and loss is not always so easy to calculate.

Poverty is not the only cause of demoralisation among many lone parents, for by no means all are particularly poor. Even when a parent is working, however, or has an adequate income, there is commonly a sense of isolation in childrearing without a partner. Although in practice the care of children in a nuclear family tends to fall overwhelmingly to one parent – usually the mother – the existence of a partner can provide some relief. Lone parents describe graphically the unremitting pressure of an unshared burden, the absence of emotional support and of even minimal help with the physical work, the lack of anyone to talk over problems with. There are facilities for lone parents that can do much to mitigate their isolation, and these are widely used, but for many lone parents the solution to their lonely role is to share it with someone in marriage (Colletta, 1983; Crosbie-Burnett, 1989).

As well as the often joyless nature of their lives, there is a second set of encouragements to marriage or remarriage in the form of widely held beliefs, shared by many lone parents, about the right way to live. There is a widespread view in Western societies that the nuclear family is the proper setting in which to bring up children (Dalley, 1988; Smart, 1984), and this is in part a reflection of the actual state of things. The large majority of dependent children in these societies live with both biological parents, and the situation of the majority is readily graced with moral approval. As a result, there is a tendency for minority arrangements like lone-parent families to be seen as something of an affront to established beliefs about family life. If such families can be seen to 'work', they undermine the credibility of the nuclear family, and this has subversive implications for the dominant economic and moral order which to a great extent depends on the nuclear family and in its turn endorses it (see, for example, Renvoize, 1985, for examples of subversive thoughts). It serves the ideological requirements of dominant groups in society to depict lone-parent families as nothing more than spoiled versions of nuclear families, and to create the belief that relationships within lone-parent households are impaired replicas of those in 'proper' families.

All this creates a climate of blame which many lone parents experience as a pressure to regularise their lives and to create a 'proper' two-parent home for their children. Burgoyne and Clark's (1984) study of step-families in Sheffield showed that a common purpose was the wish to re-create and inhabit a 'real' family – by which was meant an imitation nuclear family. There is, moreover, another element to the ideology that is relevant – the poor image of lone-parent households (except those headed by widows or widowers). There is no shortage of comments, mostly hostile, about the quality of life in lone-parent families and households.

Since over 90 per cent of lone parents are women, such comments have tended to concentrate on the supposed drawbacks for children of life without a father. Gilder (1981), for example, constructs a wide-ranging theory to explain the supposed psychological and moral disadvantages of the absence of a man in the household, and argues that fatherless boys will typically become delinquent, indolent and emotionally passive because they have no male figure on whom to model themselves and from whom to learn the economic and ethical realities of life. Similarly, Morgan (in Anderson and Davison, 1986) enters a spirited defence of fathers, mainly in the service of an anti-feminist polemic but involving predictions of the dire consequences for children who are brought up by a mother on her own. And alongside such views must be set the periodic outbursts from politicians bemoaning the spread of lone-parent families, and predicting catastrophe in the body politic if it is not checked (though people holding this view tend to be a bit coy on how this check might be brought about).

Such strictures on lone parents find only weak and ambiguous support in the available empirical evidence. It is true, certainly, that children from lone-parent households are disproportionately likely to become delinquent, but this applies to the children of divorced parents, not to the children of widows and widowers, which means that it is not the single fact of being in a lone-parent family that explains delinquency (West and Farrington, 1973). Lone-parent households are massively over-represented among social security claimants (Millar, 1989), so it makes just as much sense to look to poverty as an explanation for delinquency as to seek to blame lone parenthood. It is also probable that systems of juvenile justice, such as the British one, that encourage flexibility and discretion on the part of police officers and others in whether or not to take a young offender to court, will work against lone-parent households, and inflate their presence among delinquent populations.

The supposed tendency of children – usually, of course, boys – to become delinquent cannot therefore be taken as incontrovertible evidence that lone-parent households are bad places in which to grow up (West, 1982). Surveys of life in lone-parent families (Bachrach, 1983; Lamb, 1982; Macklin, 1980) also fail to bear out the prophets of doom. Rather, they point to the general conclusion that the adverse experiences of some children in lone-parent households are more the consequences of the events that led up to their present situation – notably the pain and uncertainty of divorce, and the economic circumstances of their present life – than of any necessary shortcomings in the emotional lives of lone-parent households (Furstenberg *et al.*, 1983; Wallerstein, 1984).

In view of this equivocal evidence, the supposed drawbacks of life for children in a lone-parent household may be viewed with some scepticism. At the same time, the supposed benefits of life in a nuclear family must also be kept in perspective. It is a pity that the discussion cannot be purged of considerations of better and worse, because they get in the way of understanding by leading to the overstated defences of the nuclear family as a God-given domestic arrangement without problems, or to the equally overstated criticisms of it as the source of all our contemporary tribulations. Human life cannot sensibly be thought of in terms of such clear-cut alternatives. Its nature is more elliptical and incoherent, and it is at best a case of minimising the drawbacks of anything within it rather than looking for perfection.

Anyone who lives or has lived in a nuclear family – which means most people in industrial societies – knows full well that the notion of the nuclear family as a 'proper' ideal is a ridiculous simplification. Many – perhaps most – adults have mixed feelings towards their parents, and believe that they have somehow, despite their best efforts and intentions, made their children's life less happy than it could have been. This suggests that the nuclear family may be the best we can manage as a means of bringing up children, but there is no point in claiming or implying that it is much of a best. The divorce rate in most industrial societies is a testimony to the personal misery that the nuclear family involves for many adults (Chester, 1977b), while the growing evidence of the incidence of brutality towards children, and of sexual attacks upon them, makes nonsense of any complacency about the nuclear family.

DILEMMAS FOR LONE PARENTS

Although a detached analysis might lead to the conclusion that there is nothing intrinsically wrong with lone-parent households and that the nuclear family is not all it is cracked up to be, such an analysis is likely to get crowded out by the pressures of life in such families. In any event, it is clear that the ideological pressure combines with the practical and emotional drawbacks of lone parenthood to make marriage or remarriage seem a beguiling prospect for many lone parents, even for those whose earlier experiences might have put them off. For many lone-parent families, therefore, their situation is recognised as an interim one, awaiting ultimate transformation into a step-family, and when a lone parent meets someone and falls in love, prudence is liable to be overwhelmed by the discomfort of the present situation and the prospect of consolation in a new relationship. Even when 'love' means little more than a tepid preference for one person over another, or even a pragmatic 'he'll do' identification of a potential partner, it is liable to be highly persuasive in the circumstances in which many lone parents find themselves; when there is a more passionate romance involved, it is likely to be irresistible. There is no reason to suppose that this range of emotions and experiences covered by the word 'love' is not also typical of marrying couples as a whole, particularly for that part of society which identifies romantic love as the basis for the choice of partner.

The way in which romance combines with a willingness to be persuaded out of an uncomfortable current situation forms an equation which is unique to each individual. It seems commonly true to say, however, that the decision by a lone parent to marry or remarry is often unduly predicated on the perceived drawbacks of life as it is. It would be impertinent to discount the difficulties of life for lone parents, but it might nevertheless be argued that there are advantages in their situation that are as real as any likely to be found in marriage, but these have to be exchanged for others when a person sets up house with someone new. There are drawbacks in most forms of domestic life, and marriage involves trading one set of advantages and disadvantages for another; for most people this trade is probably broadly advantageous, since most marriages do not end in divorce, though for lone parents the balance sheet is not the same as it is for young couples setting up house for the first time.

We need, therefore, to consider how far the discomforts of life in a lone-parent household are balanced against its compensations, many of which are likely to be lost on marriage or remarriage (Richards, 1989). Two important compensations stand out. First, there is the measure of independence that many lone parents greatly relish – not independence in the sense of freedom to come and go at will, for no parent has that, but the control over decisions that comes from needing to refer only to the well-being of family members, not to someone else's opinions. The point at which this independence becomes mere loneliness varies with individuals, but it is reported as a considerable advantage in their situation by many lone parents, as Shaw's chapter in this volume (Chapter 8) confirms.

Second, there are capacities for personal development in lone-parent households that may not be so readily available in nuclear families. The personal autonomy that lone parents may enjoy is an example of this, and of something that may have to be relinquished on marriage. For many lone mothers it is far from welcome – and a diminishing experience – to have coped so well for so long, and then to have a bossy man wading in, expecting to take over. Similarly, many lone fathers have taken on roles that are usually associated with mothering, and experience a cramping of their capabilities when a woman arrives and slips into the mothering role, excluding the man from a fulfilling aspect of daycare (George and Wilding, 1972; O'Brien, 1987).

CONFLICTING IDEOLOGIES

Whatever the personal balance of benefit and cost in each case, the fact is that lone parents marry and remarry in large numbers (Haskey, 1983). To the extent that ideological factors are at work in the process they operate in two ways: pointing the individual towards the nuclear family and pushing them away from the stigmatised state of lone parenthood. When these pressures are compounded by romantic inclinations and an uncomfortable existing life, they are liable to become peremptory. In an important sense, though, a lone parent who marries is in many cases simply doing what most marrying people do – fulfilling a destiny that had been taken for granted almost from birth. To the extent that many lone parents are simply doing what everyone else does – namely, getting married – they can be said to have their behaviour governed by the ideology of the nuclear family and the belief that a nuclear family is the correct domestic setting.

A lone parent's decision to marry, however, is not that simple. There are other people – the children – who are now part of the equation, and their needs and wishes are involved even if they are not always taken into account. The presence of children is also a factor for their parent's new partner, who may be similarly carrying out a well-understood ideological precept to be married but whose image of marriage will not have included a partner with children already in tow. At one level, then, both marriage and remarriage have a simple relationship to the dominant ideology, in that people do what everyone else does because that is the right thing to do. The particular situation of lone parents, however, brings into play other, conflicting, ideological demands – those that relate to parenthood.

Motherhood is probably more ideologically conspicuous than fatherhood, but both parental roles are heavily affected by societal expectations and internalised images. These images are often completely unreal: the sentimentalisation of young motherhood, for example, is grotesquely at odds with the exhausting demoralisation and social isolation which many mothers of young children experience (Boulton, 1983; Graham, 1980; Tivers, 1985). Nevertheless, the way parents are supposed to behave and feel is coherently enough presented for parents to be in little doubt about what is expected of them – and how far short most of them fall.

A lone parent, then, is in conflicting ideological positions. On the one hand, there is the expectation that being married is the correct thing for an adult in our society – particularly for women, who comprise most lone parents. On the other hand, there is the expectation that as parents they will subordinate their private desires and aspirations to those of their children – that they will be a mother first and a woman second. This dilemma is sharpened by the negative image of step-families, which have a reputation as troublesome (Ganong and Coleman, 1983), and this means that there is an implicit abnegation of parental responsibility in even contemplating taking one's children into such a household. Evidence exists both of the widespread recognition of this reputation, and of the fact that step-families themselves are acutely conscious of it (Sardanis-Zimmerman, 1977; Schulman, 1972).

In terms of public attitudes and the ideologies underlying them, lone parents are faced with a choice of the frying-pan or the fire, for lone parents and step-parents enjoy little public respect. The blameworthy image of step-families has a different basis from that of lone-parent families, however, and the difference will be seen to have some importance in the daily lives of both sorts of families. The generally poor esteem in which step-families are held is well documented (Coleman and Ganong, 1987). They are widely believed to conform to the traditional stereotype of cruel and neglectful settings, and there is evidence that such prejudices are held by people whose profession it is to work with families, and who might therefore be expected to be more open-minded about domestic arrangements that are different from the majority (Bryan *et al.*, 1985). Certainly such professionals should be familiar with the extensive evidence that shows that notwithstanding the difficulties that step-families encounter, for the most part they seem able to overcome these, and are on the whole indistinguishable from biological families in terms of social adjustment and domestic harmony (Bachrach, 1983; Duberman, 1975; Ferri, 1984; Ganong and Coleman, 1984).

I have argued that the antipathy towards lone-parent households is partly a reflection of a dominant ideology about the correct way to bring up children. Step-families also do not fit the ideal, and this is probably the basis for much of the hostility towards them. There is, however, a more fundamental way in which step-families apparently undermine the nuclear family, and that is the way in which they cut across assumptions about kinship. Nuclear families are predicated on the existence of a blood-tie as the fundamental defining element in domestic relationships, and kinship is so much part of our lives and system of values that we tend to take it for granted. Our personal relationships are to a large extent defined by kinship, and claims on our affections by children and parents, by brothers and sisters, and more weakly by cousins, uncles and aunts, dominate much of our subjective experience (Bahr and Nye, 1974; Farber, 1977). It is generally assumed that kinship carries with it special emotional expectations and obligations, and that relationships with people to whom we have no blood-tie – with the notable exception of spouses – are going on the whole to be less intimate, even more hostile, than relationships deriving from a blood relationship.

The lone parent who is considering marriage, therefore, faces a perplexing balance of biographical and ideological claims and pressures. Ideological imperatives are in conflict. One set points to the importance of life in the nuclear family and disdains lone parenthood; another criticises step-families by extolling parenthood and the claims of kinship. In personal terms, a lone parent cannot expect the uncomplicated enjoyment of a love affair, for the attractions of a potential partner become refracted by these ideological issues. The decision is further confused by the contradictory elements in domestic life, for the loneliness and deprivations of a person's present existence have to be set against the costs of life with a new partner, which will involve losing some of the unique advantages of lone parenthood. In view of such a complexity of issues and feelings, it is hardly surprising that remarriage and its consequences are often not straightforward, and it is worth examining how far these dilemmas manage to work themselves out.

CHILDREN IN REMARRIAGE

Adults have, at least notionally, control over their affairs and decisions. The same is not true of their children, and when we come to what happens to them in the process of the marriage of their parent, all this talk of ideology may perhaps seem inappropriate. Children, too, are sometimes influenced by the ideologies of marriage and parenthood. It is common, for example, for a teenager who is having a fraught relationship with a step-parent to blame it on the fact that the step-parent is not his or her 'real' parent, rather than notice that most of his or her contemporaries are having similar troubles at home (Lutz, 1983) and that it is adolescence, not the 'stepness' of the family, that may be the significant feature (Crosbie-Burnett, 1984). This said, though, when considering what happens to children in the vicissitudes of their parents' relationships, we need to be especially wary that we do not engage in heartless theorising. The emotional prices that life exacts cannot usefully be dismissed by glib analyses of the intrusion of ideologies into our daily experiences. Children who are involved in all or part of the sequence of divorce, lone parenthood and remarriage will commonly encounter events and emotions that are outside the experience of most children living in an intact biological family, and it is pointless to deny that many of these events and emotions are of a sort that children should be protected from. The most important of these emotions is that of loss.

Children who have lived through divorce have had to cope with loss – loss of relationships with people; loss of familiar patterns of daily life; loss, perhaps, of friends and familiar surroundings if they move house; loss of personal spaces and private associations with objects and places; loss of a sense of how the world is and of childish certainties and beliefs (Collins, 1988; Draughton, 1975; Parish and Kappes, 1980). It is no exaggeration to say that many children in divorce experience a bereavement from which it takes years to recover, and that they show many of the characteristics associated with bereavement when they become depressed and preoccupied (Wallerstein and Kelly, 1980). Often their parents are experiencing the same thing, for many people involved in divorce have very mixed feelings about it and mourn the loss of home, of relationships, of their hopes and expectations, for all that they are on balance glad to be out of their marriage.

The difference, though, is that adults are usually better able than children to understand the situation and are able to explain things, to console themselves with the prospect of freedom or a new love, with recalling the shortcomings of their erstwhile partner, with a host of sustaining beliefs and arguments that commonly succeed in offsetting the sadness enough for the adults to get by. In the case of at least one adult in divorce, the parent with whom the children continue to live, there is the additional help to be had from the urgent necessity of keeping going for their sake, the impossibility of going to pieces because their daily needs are too important, the adrenalin that concern for them can generate, the comfort of their company, the reason for living that they provide. (There is no denying, of course, that all these consolations are often short-term palliatives which are not necessarily conducive to the long-term psychological well-being of the parent, whose own needs in terms of grieving and of recovering from the pain that they have lived through are liable to be put aside while the children are cared for.)

In identifying the emotional – and in some cases practical – tasks faced by children in divorce, it is not my intention to preach to parents and suggest that they should endure a life of personal misery in order to spare their children. Everyone has to endure loss: life is mutable, a relentless round of separations which ends in the loss of life itself, and we must all deal with this as best we can. In a secular age, that usually means as much stoicism as one can manage and a commitment to make the best of what are necessarily ephemeral pleasures. This very ephemerality, though, sharpens our sense of the importance of childhood, and requires us to do what we can to preserve children from the sadness and ugliness of adult life, which they are going to encounter soon enough.

Quite often, of course, the best form of such protection is to get children away from a particular parent, and there is no doubt that many children are immeasurably better off in a lone-parent household, and that talk of bereavement is a bit fanciful when a child has been freed, perhaps, from the violence of a father, or from his sexual predatoriness. But even in such cases we need to remember that emotions are often mixed, and combined with the relief a child may still feel regret, and often guilt that he or she has split up the family. And we also need to remember the common tendency to idealise what has been lost, and to recognise that children often preserve very distorted memories of an absent parent, and consequently experience all the pain of loss despite the reality of their treatment at the hands of that parent.

As a lone-parent household evolves into a step-family, the

theme and experience of loss are often resurrected, though the detailed working out of this will vary enormously according to circumstances, especially the ages of the children involved (Goetting, 1982; Papernow, 1984). When we have lost something, we are usually wary of it happening again, and new losses, or the threat of them, are often enough to revive the pain of the former loss, even though the pain may by then have faded. People in lone-parent households put together a set of relationships, often more intimate and private than those in nuclear families, and these very precious relationships are threatened by the arrival of a step-parent. Where a lone-parent household has come about through divorce, these new relationships, created out of the wreckage of previous ones, embody a hard-won stability and sense of the meaning and purpose of life, and all this is put in jeopardy by the remarriage, so as well as the loss of actual relationships children are faced with a threat to their view of the world that may already have been challenged when the original marriage broke up. When a parent remarries, the world, made or remade, of the lone-parent household is lost, and has to be re-created using the new material, and with an inevitable adjustment – dilution – of relationships (Clingempeel *et al.*, 1984; Pasley, 1987; Simon, 1964).

THE COSTS TO LONE PARENTS

A lone parent's decision to marry incorporates an almost impossible dilemma in both ideological and personal terms. Inhabiting a role that is often ideologically frowned upon, a lone parent is nevertheless a parent, a role that carries ideological prescriptions of its own. The complex moral and practical decision to marry is not carried through in abstract contemplation, though, but is embroiled in the emotional and practical needs and demands of the people involved. The result is a compromise between competing claims and, as in most human concerns, exacts a price, ideological and emotional, from everyone involved. Some of the costs to the children have already been mentioned, and whether the cost is on balance favourable depends on individual circumstances, though research evidence suggests that it very often is (Knaub *et al.*, 1984). For lone parents entering remarriage the advantages in prospect outweigh the disadvantages, though I have argued that the decision to marry is often based more on the drawbacks of life as it is than on any very dispassionate perusal of the potential balance sheet. There is some evidence pointing to the conclusion that for many lone parents, marriage may not be the most prudent option. Remarried people, for example, are more likely to get divorced than people in their first marriage, and levels of marital satisfaction in remarriages are not on the whole as high as they are in first marriages (White and Booth, 1985). Such data mask huge ranges of experiences, and would certainly be an unreliable basis for any individual decision, but it is unmistakably clear that many lone parents might well be better off as they are rather than marrying. In short, in many cases the costs will outweigh the benefits.

I suggested that the two advantages of lone parenthood were independence and opportunities for personal development – both relative advantages, of course, but distinctive features of lone parenthood compared with parenthood in a nuclear family. Both are liable to be severely restricted or overwhelmed on marriage. To take independence first: it is inevitably a mixed blessing, and for many lone parents it is something they are glad to see the back of. 'Now I can get drunk at last' was one lone mother's comment on her marriage, meaning that now she could have a temporary respite from responsibility. Relinquishing full control, however, ushers in one of the most difficult consequences of marriage, for it raises inescapable questions of power and authority.

Domestic power and authority are not easily portable, and cannot be handed over just because a lone parent is worn out with them. Moreover, they are contaminated by ideological elements that once again have the potential to cause havoc as the lineaments of the new marriage and family begin to develop. A common example is that of children, particularly older ones, who often have a measure of power over decisions in lone-parent households that is less usual in nuclear families (Glenwick and Mowrey, 1986). The popular wisdom, though, is that men dominate the decision-making in the household and are generally in charge, and the work of Crosbie-Burnett and Giles-Sims has shown how challenging the arrival of a stepfather can be because of this (Crosbie-Burnett and Giles-Sims, forthcoming; Giles-Sims and Crosbie-Burnett, forthcoming). Ideology dictates that he seeks a role in the household which is at odds with the domestic power previously achieved by his teenage stepchildren – and all this by someone who is not 'my real father' – with the result that the adjustments required of everyone in the new household are made more difficult by ideological prescriptions about male power.

In a step-family, in other words, issues of authority and discipline, complicated enough by any standards in all families, are made even more confused by the penetration of ideological considerations. Of these, perhaps the most important is the notion of kinship, and the attendant idea that being related to someone by blood entails automatic rights and responsibilities. This puts a crucial gloss on issues of discipline, for when a step-parent enters a household, she – or more usually he – is unlikely to have his disciplinary endeavours accepted without question by the children because he will not be seen to have the moral authority that goes with being related to someone (Stern, 1978). In other words, a biological parent who attempts to discipline and control children starts with the advantage of a generally sanctioned right to do it, and a general expectation that he or she will. Welcome as the prospect of a break from single-handed responsibilities is to many lone parents, the relief may be dearly bought.

A second distinct strength of lone-parent families was the opportunity to accomplish parental roles that are liable to be divided along gender lines in nuclear families. Many lone mothers value the experience of doing things that are traditionally the preserve of men, and for lone fathers the partial adoption of traditionally maternal responsibilities is a congenial part of parenting. Although many of these activities are mundane enough – things like unblocking sinks and doing the ironing – and although there is no reason why they need to be allocated along gender lines in nuclear families, they were a source of pride to many of the parents with whose experiences this chapter is concerned, and there is a growing belief that most children would benefit from seeing the breakdown of the usual division of labour, and having the experience of being brought up by a man with the space and opportunity to develop the gentler aspects of his personality and character in his relationship with them, or by a woman who is less passive than she is traditionally encouraged to be. With marriage, there is a danger that some of the sense of achievement in doing non-traditional parts of parenting may be lost. Marriage can, therefore, be a diminishing experience in this respect, because it may cramp the capabilities of lone parents and restrict their personal development if domestic and parental responsibilities are shared along routine gender lines. Yet resisting such a process is likely to involve a deliberate confrontation with ideological precepts, and may clash with the aspiration to be a 'proper' family.

There is some evidence that step-families are often not very cohesive (Pill, 1990). There may be a number of biographical reasons for this, notably the relationship between the children and their non-residential parent, which works against establishing a solid emotional boundary around a household (Boss and Greenberg, 1984). As well as such essentially practical factors, there is often a major ideological reason why a reconstituted family is less close-knit than the lone-parent household that went before, and that is the absence of kinship as the defining characteristic of cross-generational relationships within the household (Whiteside, 1989).

A lone parent who marries enters a world in which there are new rules. In nuclear families the broad purpose and the rules are roughly understood, though obviously they will be renegotiated in individual cases. In step-families the rules are by no means so ready-made, and traditional parental roles are not always easy to adapt because of the lack of the element of kinship. Women, for example, are expected to feel motherly and to behave with tenderness to their children, though they are also permitted a measure of exasperation, and nobody intervenes when a mother 'smacks' – hits – her child in a supermarket. But tenderness and motherly feelings are assumed to belong with biological motherhood, and a stepmother is faced with this assumption, and the related one that relationships not based on kinship will be cooler and more distant than those that are. Similarly, to the extent that discipline is traditionally a male preserve, there is little doubt that kinship sanctions aspects of discipline, and probably makes them more acceptable to children.

There is widespread agreement among writers on step-families that it is asking for trouble for an incoming step-parent to embrace the parental role defined for him or her by the usual expectations of society (Collins, 1988; Visher and Visher, 1979), and it follows that adults have no choice but to evolve a relationship with children towards whom society has identified no role and defined no set of feelings. When such ideological factors become mixed up in emotional considerations, especially those of loss, a highly delicate task faces everyone in turn. Ideologically prescribed parental roles are in conflict with the demands and legitimations of kinship, and all this has then to be played out in a household where there is frequently a lot of anger as a result of perceived losses, sometimes a fair measure of apathy deriving from those losses and the attendant depression, as well as from a caution bred of insecurity associated with past disappointments in relationships. This is hardly the most propitious environment in which to start to construct the working relationships of a household, let alone the affectionate ones of a family.

CONCLUSION

In this chapter, I have tried to draw out a few themes from the congeries of issues that affect lone parents. I have argued that the poor reputation of lone-parent families is a feature of the dominant ideology of Western societies, which is expressed in an idealisation of the nuclear family and a contempt for alternatives that might represent a challenge to this image of nuclear family life. These ideological concerns affect the daily lives of families – partly through the critical image of themselves which lone-parent households find it hard to ignore, partly in the colouring of crucial decisions. One such decision is whether or whom to marry, and this carries heavy ideological overtones, notably the conflicting prescriptions that people should marry and live in a 'real' family, but that parenthood requires one to subordinate one's private aspirations to the needs of one's children.

Negotiating this dilemma is not made easier by the poverty and loneliness that many lone parents experience, which are likely to pull many of them towards marriage as a solution. Real as the drawbacks of lone parenthood are, though, they may sometimes be offset by the advantages of a lone parent's life, notably the independence and the ability to enjoy aspects of parenting that are less readily available in two-parent households. Such advantages are commonly sacrificed with marriage, but the decision about whether such a sacrifice is justified is liable to be contaminated by the ideological pressures which bear down on lone-parent households. A realistic assessment of the prospects of happiness is therefore made harder by the ideological climate in which it must be made.

Life, however, is not a matter of enacting an ideology, but of feelings and experiences that are important in their own right, for all that they are influenced by and played out against an ideological background. I have been concerned to stress the reality and importance of the feelings of people, particularly children, and the need to respect these, even though we also try to understand them in their ideological context. I have argued that the important factor for children living through divorce is the loss of existing patterns of relationships, of ways of life and beliefs about the world and about adult relationships, and that many children in these circumstances are experiencing something indistinguishable from bereavement. With the marriage of a parent, some of these losses are repeated, new losses are experienced, and memories of previous losses revived; and similar feelings are also likely in children whose parent is marrying for the first time. Because loss is an inescapable part of life, all this may be unavoidable, but the reality for the people involved should not therefore be underestimated.

With the marriage of a parent, adjustments have to be made which are not helped either by the children's likely state of mind and feeling after the losses they have experienced, or by the new ideological climate that has been entered. Step-families have an unfavourable public image, explicable in part by the premium put on kinship in Western societies – and indeed in most societies – and by the hostility towards forms of personal relationship other than those based on kinship. This emphasis on kinship undermines the moral authority of step-parents and makes their affectionate overtures to children seem meretricious, so it has a direct influence on the quality of daily domestic life.

As well as finding their way through such issues, remarried couples have to define their roles, and here again personal factors are liable to be in conflict with ideological factors, for there are ideological assumptions that dictate how parents should conduct themselves – notably how their labour in the home should be divided, with women doing the caring and men doing the breadwinning and the domestic discipline. Such prescriptions, however, will often be in conflict with the claims of the residues of life in the lone-parent household, in which lone parents perforce double up many of these roles. The consequence is that new step-families typically experience strain as the lone parent relinquishes – or is invited to relinquish – roles which he or she may have found a particularly satisfying part of lone parenthood.

It has not been my object in this chapter to advise lone parents on whether or not to marry, but to highlight the complexities involved. Empirical evidence is fairly reassuring in indicating that many step-families negotiate the difficulties well enough, but it also shows that lone-parent households are far less unsatisfactory environments for children than public rhetoric, generally from the political right, seeks to convey. By contrasting some aspects of life in lone-parent families with that in step-families, though, we are able to identify some of the strengths of lone-parent households. They are often places in which parents who perform both parental roles are able to develop parts of their personalities that are liable to have less scope in nuclear families. They are also places in which high levels of intimacy and affection have been achieved out of the remnants of a destroyed nuclear family, and this is put at risk by moving into a step-family. There are advantages to offset the losses, but whether these are a fair exchange is a matter for individual assessment in each particular instance, and it is important that such assessment is not overwhelmed by the drawbacks of life in a lone-parent household, nor by the demands of prevailing ideologies.

Bibliography

Abbott, P. and Wallace, C. (1989), 'The Family', in P. Brown and R. Sparks (eds), *Beyond Thatcherism: Social policy, politics and society*, Milton Keynes: Open University Press.

Abercrombie, N., Warde, A. with Soothhill, K., Urry, J. and Walby, S. (1988), *Contemporary British Society: A new introduction to sociology*, Cambridge: Polity Press.

Allan, G. (1985), *Family Life: Domestic roles and social organization*, Oxford: Basil Blackwell.

Allan, G. (1989), *Friendship: Developing a sociological perspective*, Hemel Hempstead: Harvester Wheatsheaf.

Allen, Y. (1987), *Successfully Single, Successfully Yourself*, London: Cedar.

Anderson, D. and Davison, G. (eds) (1986), *Family Portraits*, London: The Social Affairs Unit.

Arber, S., Gilbert, G. and Dale, A. (1985), 'Paid employment and women's health: A benefit or a source of role strain?', *Sociology of Health and Illness*, 7, 3: 375–400.

Archbishop of Canterbury's Commission on Urban Priority Areas (1985), *Faith in the City: A call for action by church and nation*, London: Church House.

Arendell, T. (1986), *Mothers and Divorce: Legal, economic and social dilemmas*, Berkeley, CA: University of California Press.

Ashley, P. (1983), *The Money Problems of the Poor*, London: Heinemann.

Audirac, P. (1986), 'La Cohabitation', *Economie et Statistique*, **185**: 13–33.

Austerberry, H. and Watson, S. (1985), 'A woman's place: A feminist approach to housing in Britain', in C. Ungerson (ed.), *Women and Social Policy: A reader*, London and Basingstoke: Macmillan.

Bachrach, C.A. (1983), 'Children in families: Characteristics of biological, step-children and adopted children', *Journal of Marriage and the Family*, **45**: 171–9.

Bahr, H.M. and Nye, F.I. (1974), 'The kinship role in a contemporary community: Perceptions of obligations and sanctions', *Journal of Comparative Family Studies*, **5**: 17–25.

Baker, J. (1986), 'Comparing national priorities: Family and population policy in Britain and France', *Journal of Social Policy*, **15**, 4: 421–42.

Barrett, M. and McIntosh, M. (1982), *The Anti-Social Family*, London: Verso.

Bastide, H., Girard A. and Roussel, L. (1982), 'Une enquête d'opinion sur la conjuncture démographique', *Population*, **37**: 904–20.

Beatson-Hird, P., Yuen, P. and Balarajan, R. (1989), 'Single mothers: Their health and health service use', *Journal of Epidemiology and Community Health*, **43**: 385–90.

Becker, H.S. (1970), *Sociological Work: Method and substance*, Chicago: Aldine.

Beechey, V. and Perkins, T. (1987), *A Matter of Hours: Women, part-time work and the labour market*, Cambridge: Polity Press.

Beltram, G. (1984), *Testing the Safety Net*, London: Bedford Square Press/National Council for Voluntary Organizations.

Benveniste, C. and Lollivier, S. (1988), 'Les écarts de salaire entre les hommes et les femmes continuent à se réduire', *Economie et Statistique*, **210**: 3–9.

Bernard, J. (1973), *The Future of Marriage*, London: Souvenir.

Bernardes, J. (1985), 'Do we really know what "the family" is?', in P. Close and R. Collins (eds), *Family and Economy in Modern Society*, London and Basingstoke: Macmillan.

Berthoud, R. (1985), *The Examination of Social Security*, London: Policy Studies Institute.

Berthoud, R. and Brown, J.C. with Cooper, S. (1981), *Poverty and the Development of Anti-Poverty Policy in the United Kingdom*, London: Heinemann.

Beveridge, W. (1942), *Report on Social Insurance and Allied Services*, Cmnd 6404, London: HMSO.

Blaxter, M. (1990), *Health and Lifestyles*, London: Tavistock/Routledge.

Blumer, H. (1969), *Symbolic Interactionism: Perspectives and method*, Englewood Cliffs, NJ: Prentice Hall.

Bohannan, P. (1970), 'The six stations of divorce', in P. Bohannan (ed.), *Divorce and After*, New York: Doubleday.

Boigeol, A., Commaille, J. and Munoz-Perez, B. (1984), 'Le divorce' in *Données Sociales*, Paris: Institut National de la Statistique et des Etudes Economiques.

Bolden, K. (1980), 'The morbidity of single parent families', *Journal of Maternal and Child Health*, **5**, June: 256–60.

Boss, P. and Greenberg, J. (1984), 'Family boundary ambiguity: A new variable in family stress theory', *Family Process*, **23**, 4: 535–46.

Boudon, R. (1988), *The Analysis of Ideology*, Cambridge: Polity Press.

Boudoul, J. and Faur, J.P. (1987), 'Trente ans de migration intérieure', in *Données Sociales*, Paris: Institut National de la Statistique et des Etudes Economiques.

Boulton, M. (1983), *On Being a Mother: A study of women with pre-school children*, London: Tavistock.

Bradshaw, J. (1989), *Lone Parents: Policy in the doldrums*, London: Family Policy Studies Centre.

Brailey, M. (1985), 'Making the break', in N. Johnson (ed.), *Marital Violence*, London: Routledge & Kegan Paul.

Bramall, M. (1975), 'The National Council for One Parent Families', in D. Barber (ed.), *One Parent Families*, London: Davies Poynter.

Brannen, J. and Moss, P. (1988), *New Mothers at Work: Employment and childcare*, London: Unwin Hyman.

Brannen, J. and Wilson, G. (eds) (1987), *Give and Take in Families: Studies in resource distribution*, London: Allen & Unwin.

Braybon, G. and Summerfield, P. (1987), *Women's Experience in Two World Wars*, London: Pandora.

Brown, J.C. (1983), *Family Income Supplement*, London: Policy Studies Institute.

Brown, J.C. (1988), *In Search of a Policy: The rationale for social security provision for one parent families*, London: National Council for One Parent Families.

Brownfain, J. (1985), 'A study of the married bisexual male: Paradox and resolution', in F. Klein and T. Wolf (eds), *Bisexualities: Theory and research*, New York: Haworth.

Bryan, H., Ganong, L., Coleman, M. and Bryan, L. (1985), 'Counselors' perceptions of stepparents and stepchildren', *Journal of Counseling Psychology*, **32**, 2: 279–82.

Bryant, C. and Wells, D. (1973), *Deviancy in the Family*, Philadelphia: F.A. Davis.

Bulmer, M. (1989), 'The underclass, empowerment and public policy', in M. Bulmer, J. Lewis and D. Piachaud (eds), *The Goals of Social Policy*, London: Unwin Hyman.

Burgoyne, J. (1984), *Breaking Even: Divorce, your children and you*, Harmondsworth: Penguin.

Burgoyne, J. (1987), 'Rethinking the family life cycle: Sexual divisions, work and domestic life in the post-war period', in A. Bryman, B. Bytheway, P. Allatt and T. Keil (eds), *Rethinking the Life Cycle*, London and Basingstoke: Macmillan.

Burgoyne, J. and Clark, D. (1984), *Making a Go of It: A study of stepfamilies in Sheffield*, London: Routledge & Kegan Paul.

Burgoyne, J., Ormrod, R. and Richards, M. (1987), *Divorce Matters*, Harmondsworth: Penguin.

Burnell, I. and Wadsworth, J. (1981), 'Children in one parent families: The effects on children of changing family status at birth to age five', *Child Health Research Unit, Department of Child Health*, University of Bristol.

Burnell, I. and Wadsworth, J. (1982), 'Home truths', *One Parent Times*, **8**: 8–12.

Byrne, D. (1989), *Beyond the Inner City*, Milton Keynes: Open University Press.

Cashmore, E.E. (1985), *Having To: The world of one parent families*, London: Counterpoint.

Central Statistical Office (1987), *Social Trends*, London: HMSO.

Centre d'Etude des Revenus et des Coûts (CERC) (1979), *Rapport sur les Revenus des Français*, Paris: Editions Albatros.

Champion, T. (1989), 'Internal migration and the spatial distribution of population', in H. Joshi (ed.), *The Changing Population of Britain*, Oxford: Basil Blackwell.

Chester, R. (1977a), 'The one parent family: Deviant or variant?', in R. Chester and J. Peel (eds), *Equalities and Inequalities in Family Life*, London: Academic Press.

Chester, R. (ed.) (1977b), *Divorce in Europe*, Leiden: Nijhoff.

Chilman, C.S. (1988), 'Never-married, single, adolescent parents', in C.S. Chilman, E.W. Nunnally and F.M. Cox (eds), *Variant Family Forms*, London: Sage.

Clark, W., Freeman, H., Kane, R. and Lewis, C. (1987), 'The influence of domestic position on health status', *Social Science and Medicine*, **24**, 6: 501–6.

Clingempeel, W.G., Brand, E. and Segal, S. (1987), 'A multi-level/multi-variable developmental perspective for future research on stepfamilies', in K. Pasley and M. Ihinger-Tallman (eds), *Remarriage and Stepparenting: Current research and theory*, New York: Guilford Press.

Clingempeel, W.G., Ievoli, R. and Brand, E. (1984), 'Structural complexity and the quality of stepfather/stepchild relationships', *Family Process*, **23**, 4: 547–60.

Clingempeel, W.G. and Segal, S. (1986), 'Stepparent/stepchild relationships and the psychological adjustment of children in stepmother and stepfather families', *Child Development*, **57**: 474–84.

Close, P. (1985), 'Family form and economic production', in P. Close and R. Collins (eds), *Family and Economy in Modern Society*, London and Basingstoke: Macmillan.

Cohen, B. (1988), *Caring for Children*, London: Family Policy Studies Centre.

Cohen, B. (1990): *Caring for Children: The 1990 report*, London: Family Policy Studies Centre.

Coleman, E. (1985), 'Integration of male bisexuality and marriage', in F. Klein and T. Wolf (eds), *Bisexualities: Theory and research*, New York: Haworth.

Coleman, M. and Ganong, L.H. (1987), 'The cultural stereotyping of stepfamilies', in K. Pasley and M. Ihinger-Tallman (eds), *Remarriage and Stepparenting: Current research and theory*, New York: Guilford Press.

Colletta, N.D. (1983), 'Stressful lives: The situation of divorced mothers and their children', *Journal of Divorce*, **6**, 3: 19–31.

Collins, S. (1988), *Step-Parents and their Children*, London: Souvenir Press.

Comitato Italiano por lo studio de problemi della populazione (1982), 'Economic and social features of households in the member states of the EC', *Eurostat*, Brussels: EC.

Conseil Economique et Sociale (1987), *Grande Pauvreté et Précarité*, Journal Officiel de la République Française.

Cook, D. (1989), *Rich Law, Poor Law: Different responses to tax and supplementary benefit fraud*, Milton Keynes: Open University Press.

Cox, B.D. *et al.*, (1987), *The Health and Lifestyles Survey*, London: Health Promotion Research Trust.

Crehan, K. (1986), 'Women, work and the balancing act', in T.S. Epstein, K. Crehan, A. Gerzer and J. Sass (eds), *Women, Work and Family in Britain and Germany*, London: Croom Helm.

Crosbie-Burnett, M. (1984), 'The centrality of the step relationship: A challenge to family theory and practice', *Family Relations*, **33**: 459–63.

Crosbie-Burnett, M. (1989), 'Application of family stress theory to remarriage: A model for assessing and helping stepfamilies', *Family Relations*, **38**: 323–31.

Crosbie-Burnett, M. and Giles-Sims, J. (forthcoming), 'Marital power in step-families: A test of normative-resource theory', *Journal of Family Psychology*.

Crow, G. (1989), 'The use of the concept of "strategy" in recent sociological literature', *Sociology*, **23**: 1–24.

Crow, G. and Hardey, M. (1991, forthcoming), 'Diversity and ambiguity among lone-parent households in modern Britain', in C. Marsh and S. Arber (eds), *Household and Family: Divisions and change*, London and Basingstoke: Macmillan.

Dalley, G. (1988), *Ideologies of Caring: Rethinking community and collectivism*, London and Basingstoke: Macmillan.

David, M. and New, C. (1986), 'Feminist perspectives on childcare policy', in B. Cohen and K. Clarke (eds), *Childcare and Equal Opportunities: Some policy perspectives*, Manchester: Equal Opportunities Commission.

Davies, F. (1963), *Passage Through Crisis: Polio victims and their families*, New York: Bobbs-Merrill.

Davis, C. and Ritchie, J. (1988), *Tipping the Balance*, Joint DHSS Report No. 16, London: HMSO.

Deacon, A. and Bradshaw, J. (1983), *Reserved for the Poor: The means test in British social policy*, Oxford: Martin Robertson.

Debonneuil, M. (1978), 'Les familles pauvres d'une ville moyenne', *Economie et Statistique*.

Department of Employment (1989), *Labour Market Quarterly*, May, London: Department of Employment.

Department of Health and Social Security (1974), *Report of the Committee on One Parent Families* ('Finer Report'), London: HMSO.

Department of Health and Social Security (1985), *The Reform of Social Security: Programme for action*, London: HMSO.

Department of Social Security (1989), *Social Security Statistics 1988*, London: HMSO.

Department of Social Security (1990), *Social Security Statistics 1989*, London: HMSO.

Desplanques, G. and de Saboulin, M. (1986), 'Mariage et premier enfant: un lien qui se défait', *Economie et Statistique*, **187**: 31–45.

Deven, F. and Cliquet, R. (eds) (1986), *One Parent Families in Europe*, The Hague: Inter-University Demographic Institute.

Dex, S. (1988), *Women's Attitudes Towards Work*, London and Basingstoke: Macmillan.

Dollamore, G. (1990), 'Birth statistics 1989', *Population Trends*, **61**: 11–16.

Donnison, D. and Ungerson, C. (1982), *Housing Policy*, Harmondsworth: Penguin.

Draughton, M. (1975), 'Stepmother's model of identification in relation to mourning in the child', *Psychological Reports*, **36**, 1: 183–9.

Duberman, L. (1975), *The Reconstituted Family: A study of remarried couples and their children*, Chicago: Nelson-Hall.

Duskin, E. (1988), 'Lone parenthood and the low income trap', *OECD Observer*, **153**.

Edwards, S. and Halpern, A. (1988), 'Maintenance in 1987: Fact or fantasy?', *Family Law*, **18** (April): 117–21.

Eekelaar, J. (1984), *Family Law and Social Policy*, 2nd edn, London: Weidenfeld & Nicolson.

Eekelaar, J. and Maclean, M. (1986), *Maintenance After Divorce*, Oxford: Clarendon Press.

Elliot, F.R. (1986), *The Family: Change or continuity?*, London and Basingstoke: Macmillan.

Emerson, J. (1970), 'Nothing unusual is happening', in T. Shibutani (ed.), *Human Nature and Collective Behavior*, Englewood Cliffs, NJ: Prentice Hall.

Equal Opportunities Commission (1989), *Women and Men in Britain*, Manchester: Equal Opportunities Commission.

Equal Opportunities Commission (1990), *Action Plan for Childcare*, Manchester: Equal Opportunities Commission.

Ermisch, J. (1989), 'Divorce: Economic antecedents and aftermath', in H. Joshi (ed.), *The Changing Population of Britain*, Oxford: Basil Blackwell.

Ermisch, J. and Wright, R. (1989), 'Lone parents and employment: Theoretical issues and empirical evidence', paper given at conference on Family Life in Lone Parent Households, University of Surrey.

Essen, J. (1978), 'Living in one-parent families: Income and expenditure', *Poverty*, **40**: 23–8.

European Parliament (1986), *Report drawn up on behalf of the Committee on women's rights on one parent families*, WG(VIS) 2109E, Luxembourg.

Evason, E. (1980), *Just Me and the Kids: A study of single parent families in Northern Ireland*, Belfast Equal Opportunities Commission for Northern Ireland.

Fagin, L. and Little, M. (1984), *The Forsaken Families*, Harmondsworth: Penguin.

Farber, B. (1977), 'Social context, kinship mapping and family norms', *Journal of Marriage and the Family*, **39**: 227–40.

Ferraro, K. and Johnson, J. (1983), 'How women experience battering: Process of victimization', *Social Problems*, **30**: 325–39.

Ferri, E. (1976), *Growing Up in a One Parent Family*, Windsor: National Foundation for Educational Research.

Ferri, E. (1984), *Stepchildren: A national survey*, Windsor: National Foundation for Educational Research.

Field, F. (1989), *Losing Out: The emergence of Britain's underclass*, Oxford: Basil Blackwell.

Finch, J. (1989), *Family Obligations and Social Change*, Cambridge: Polity Press.

Ford, J. (1988), *The Indebted Society: Credit and default in the 1980s*, London: Routledge.

Forrest, R. and Murie, A. (1987a), 'The pauperisation of council housing', *Roof*, **12**, 1 (January/February) 20–3.

Forrest, R. and Murie, A. (1987b), 'The affluent homeowner: labour-market position and the shaping of housing histories', in N. Thrift and P. Williams (eds), *Class and Space: The making of urban society*, London: Routledge & Kegan Paul.

Forrest, R. and Murie, A. (1988), *Selling the Welfare State: The privatisation of public housing*, London: Routledge.

Forrest, R., Murie, A. and Williams, P. (1990), *Home Ownership: Differentiation and fragmentation*, London: Unwin Hyman.

Fournier, J.V. (1989), 'Traitement de fonctionnaires en 1988', *Economie et Statistique*, **129**: 11–29.

Fox, J. and Goldblatt, P. (1982), 'OPCS longitudinal study: Socio-demographic mortality differentials 1971–75', *Series LS, No. 1*, London: HMSO.

Fuller, R. and Stevenson, O. (1983), *Policies, Programmes and Disadvantage: A review of the literature*, London: Heinemann.

Furstenberg, F., Brooks-Gunn, J. and Morgan, S. (1987), *Adolescent Mothers in Later Life*, Cambridge: Cambridge University Press.

Furstenberg, F., Peterson, J., Windquist-Nord, C. and Zill, N. (1983), 'The life course of children and divorce: marital disruption and parental contact', *American Sociological Review*, **48**: 656–68.

Ganong, L.H. and Coleman, M. (1983), 'Step parent: A pejorative term?', *Psychological Reports*, **52**: 919–22.

Ganong, L.H. and Coleman, M. (1984), 'The effects of remarriage on children: A review of the empirical literature', *Family Relations*, **33**: 389–406.

General Household Survey (GHS) (1985), Office of Population Census and Surveys, London: HMSO.

Genovese, R.G. (1984), *Families and Change: Social needs and public policy*, South Hadley, MA: Bergin & Garvey.

George, V. and Wilding, P. (1972), *Motherless Families*, London: Routledge & Kegan Paul.

George, V. and Wilding, P. (1984), *The Impact of Social Policy*, London: Routledge & Kegan Paul.

Gilder, G. (1981), *Wealth and Poverty*, New York: Basic Books.

Giles-Sims, J. and Crosbie-Burnett, M. (forthcoming), 'Adolescent power in stepfather families: An application of normative-resource theory', *Journal of Marriage and the Family*.

Gittins, D. (1985), *The Family in Question: Changing households and familiar ideologies*, London and Basingstoke: Macmillan.

Glendinning, C. (1987), 'Impoverishing women', in A. Walker and C. Walker (eds), *The Growing Divide: A social audit 1979–1987*, London: Child Poverty Action Group.

Glendinning, C. and Millar, J. (eds) (1987), *Women and Poverty in Britain*, Hemel Hempstead: Harvester Wheatsheaf.

Glenwick, D.S. and Mowrey, J.D. (1986), 'When parent becomes peer: Loss of intergenerational boundaries in single parent families', *Family Relations*, **35**: 57–62.

Gochros, J. (1985), 'Wives' reaction to learning that their husbands are bisexual', in F. Klein and T. Wolf (eds), *Bisexualities: Theory and research*, New York: Haworth.

Gochros, J. (1989), *When Husbands Come Out of the Closet*, New York: Haworth.

Goetting, A. (1982), 'The six stages of remarriage: Developmental tasks of remarriage after divorce', *Family Relations*, **31**: 213–22.

Goode, W. (1965), *Women in Divorce*, New York: Free Press.

Gordon, T. (1990), *Feminist Mothers*, London and Basingstoke: Macmillan.

Graham, H. (1980), 'Mothers' accounts of anger and aggression towards their babies', in N. Frude (ed.), *Psychological Approaches to Child Abuse*, London: Batsford.

Graham, H. (1984), *Women, Health and the Family*, Brighton: Wheatsheaf.

Graham, H. (1987a), 'Being poor: Perceptions and coping strategies of lone mothers', in J. Brannen and G. Wilson (eds), *Give and Take in Families: Studies in resource distribution*, London: Allen & Unwin.

Graham, H. (1987b), 'Women's poverty and caring', in C. Glendinning and J. Millar (eds) (1987), *Women and Poverty in Britain*, Hemel Hempstead: Harvester Wheatsheaf.

Gray, F. (1979), 'Consumption: Council house management', in S. Merrett with F. Gray, *State Housing in Britain*, London: Routledge & Kegan Paul.

Green, E. and Hebron, S. (1988), 'Leisure and male partners', in E. Wimbush and M. Talbot (eds), *Relative Freedoms: Women and leisure*, Milton Keynes: Open University Press.

Greenblatt, C. (1983), 'The salience of sexuality in the early years of marriage', *Journal of Marriage and the Family*, **45**: 289–99.

Groves, D. (1983), 'Members and survivors: Women and retirement pensions legislation', in J. Lewis (ed.), *Women's Welfare/ Women's Rights*, London: Croom Helm.

Hardey, M. (1989), 'Lone parents and the home', in G. Allan and G. Crow (eds), *Home and Family: Creating the domestic sphere*, London and Basingstoke: Macmillan.

Harris, C.C. (1983), *The Family and Industrial Society*, London: Allen & Unwin.

Harrison, P. (1983), *Inside the Inner City: Life under the cutting edge*, Harmondsworth: Penguin.

Hart, N. (1976), *When Marriage Ends: A study in status passage*, London: Tavistock.

Hartmann, H. (1987), 'Changes in women's economic and family roles in post-World War II United States', in L. Beneria and C.R. Stimpson (eds), *Women, Households and the Economy*, New Brunswick, NJ: Rutgers University Press.

Haskey, J. (1983), 'Remarriage of the divorced in England and Wales: A contemporary phenomenon', *Journal of Biosocial Science*, **15**: 253–71.

Haskey, J. (1986), 'One-parent families in Great Britain', *Population Trends*, **45**: 5–13.

Haskey, J. (1989a), 'One-parent families and their children in Great Britain: Numbers and characteristics', *Population Trends*, **55**: 27–33.

Haskey, J. (1989b), 'Families and households of the ethnic minority and White populations of Great Britain', *Population Trends*, **57**: 8–19.

Haskey, J. (1990), 'The children of families broken by divorce', *Population Trends*, **61**: 34–42.

Henderson, J. and Karn, V. (1987), *Race, Class and State Housing: Inequality and the allocation of public housing in Britain*, Aldershot: Gower.

Hill, M. (1989), 'Income maintenance and local government: Implementing central control?', *Critical Social Policy*, **25**: 18–36.

Hipgrave, T. (1982), 'Lone fatherhood: A problematic status', in L. McKee and M. O'Brien (eds), *The Father Figure*, London: Tavistock.

HMSO (1990), *Children Come First*, London: HMSO.

HM Treasury (1989), *The Government's Expenditure Plans 1989/90 to 1991/92*, DSS Cmnd 615, London: HMSO.

Hobcraft, J. (1989), 'People and services: Central assessment of local needs', in H. Joshi (ed.), *The Changing Population of Britain*, Oxford: Basil Blackwell.

Hobcraft, J. and Joshi, H. (1989), 'Population matters', in H. Joshi (ed.), *The Changing Population of Britain*, Oxford: Basil Blackwell.

Holme, A. (1985), *Housing and Young Families in East London*, London: Routledge & Kegan Paul.

Hunt, A., Fox, J. and Morgan, M. (1973), *Families and Their Needs*, London: HMSO.

Hurstfield, J. (1978), *The Part-Time Trap*, Low Pay Unit, No. 9, London.

Hyatt, J. and Parry-Cook, G. (1990), *Barriers at Work: A study of lone parents' training and employment needs*, London: National Council for One Parent Families.

Ihinger-Tallman, M. and Pasley, K. (1987), *Remarriage*, Newbury Park, CA: Sage.

Incomes Data Services (1990), *IDS Study 472*, December.

Industrial Relations Report and Review (1RRR) (1989), Report 42 (June).

Ineichen, B. (1977), 'Youthful marriage: The vortex of disadvantage', in R. Chester and J. Peel (eds), *Equalities and Inequalities in Family Life*, London: Academic Press.

Itzin, C. (1980), *Splitting Up: Single parent liberation*, London: Virago.

Jackson, B. (1982), 'Single parent families', in R.N. Rapoport, M.P. Fogarty and R. Rapoport (eds), *Families in Britain*, London: Routledge & Kegan Paul.

Jones, G. (1987), 'Young workers in the class structure', *Work, Employment and Society*, **1**, 4: 487–508.

Jones, G.S. (1971), *Outcast London*, London: Clarendon Press.

Joshi, H. (1987), 'Obstacles and opportunities for lone parents as breadwinners in Britain', OECD Conference on Lone Parents: *The Economic Challenge of New Family Structures*, December, Paris: OECD.

Joshi, H. and Newell, R. (1987), 'Pay differences between men and women', *Discussion Paper 156*, London: Centre for Economic Policy Research.

Kamerman, S. and Kahn, A.J. (1988), *Mothers Alone*, Dover, MA: Auburn House.

Karn, V. and Henderson, J. (1983), 'Housing atypical households: Understanding the practices of local government housing', in A.W. Franklin (ed.), *Family Matters: Perspectives on the family and social policy*, Oxford: Pergamon Press.

Kessler, D. and Masson, A. (1985), 'What are the distributional consequences of the socialist government policy in France?' *Journal of Social Policy*, **14**, 3: 403–18.

Kiernan, K. (1989), 'The family: Formation and fission', in H. Joshi (ed.), *The Changing Population of Britain*, Oxford: Basil Blackwell.

Kiernan, K. and Wicks, M. (1990), *Family Change and Future Policy*, London: Family Policy Studies Centre/Joseph Rowntree Memorial Trust.

Knaub, P.K., Hanna, S.L. and Stinnett, N. (1984), 'Strengths of remarried families', *Journal of Divorce*, **7**: 41–55.

Knight, I. (1981), *Family Finances*, London: OPCS.

Kompara, D.R. (1980), 'Difficulties in the socialization process of stepparenting', *Family Relations*, **29**: 327–37.

Kowarzik, U. and Popay, J. (1988), *That's Women's Work*, London Research Centre.

Lamb, M.E. (ed.) (1982), *Non-Traditional Families*, London: Lawrence Erlbaum.

Lambert, L. and Streather, J. (1980), *Children in Changing Families*, London: Macmillan/National Children's Bureau.

Land, H. (1979), 'The boundaries between the state and the family', *The Sociology of the Family*, Sociological Review Monograph 28, London: Routledge.

Land, H. (1983), 'Who still cares for the family?', in J. Lewis (ed.), *Women's Welfare/Women's Rights*, London: Croom Helm.

Laroque, P. (1985), *La Politique familiale en France depuis 1945*, Paris: Documentation Française.

Lawson, A. (1989), *Adultery: Analysis of love and betrayal*, Oxford: Basil Blackwell.

Layard, R., Piachaud, D. and Stewart, M. (1978), 'The causes of poverty', Royal Commission on the Distribution of Income and Wealth, Background Paper No. 5, London: HMSO.

Le Gall, D. and Martin, C. (1987), *Les Familles monoparentales*, Paris: ESF.

Leonard, D. and Speakman, M. (1986), 'Women in the family: Companions or caretakers?', In V. Beechey and E. Whitelegg (eds), *Women in Britain Today*, Milton Keynes: Open University Press.

Lewis, J. (1986), 'Anxieties about the family and the relationships between parents, children and the state in twentieth-century England', in M. Richards and P. Light (eds) (1986), *Children of Social Worlds*, Cambridge: Polity Press.

Lewis, J. (1989), 'Lone parent families: Politics and economics', *Journal of Social Policy*, **18**: 595–600.

Lewis, J. and Piachaud, D. (1987), 'Women and poverty in the twentieth century', in C. Glendinning and J. Millar (eds), *Women and Poverty in Britain*, Hemel Hempstead: Harvester Wheatsheaf.

Liaisons Sociales (1989), *Mémo social*, Paris: Liaisons Sociales.

Liaisons Sociales (1990), *Barrière sociale périodique*, Paris: Liaisons Sociales.

Logan, F. (1986), *Homelessness and Relationship Breakdown*, London: National Council for One Parent Families.

Lund, M. (1984), 'Research on divorce and children', *Family Law*, **14**: 198–201.

Lutz, P. (1983), 'The step family: An adolescent perspective', *Family Relations*, **32**: 367–75.

McDowell, L. (1983), 'Housing deprivation. An intergenerational approach', in M. Brown (ed.), *The Structure of Disadvantage*, London: Heinemann.

Macintyre, S. (1977), *Single and Pregnant*, London: Croom Helm.

Macklin, E.D. (1980), 'Non-traditional family forms: A decade of research', *Journal of Marriage and the Family*, **42**, 4: 904–23.

Maclean, M. and Eekelaar, M.J. (1983), *Children and Divorce*, Oxford: SSRC/Centre for Socio-Legal Studies.

McRobbie, A. (1989), 'Motherhood, a teenage job?', *The Guardian*, 5 April, p. 17.

Mansfield, P. and Collard, J. (1988), *The Beginning of the Rest of Your Life? A Portrait of Newly-Wed Marriage*, London and Basingstoke: Macmillan.

Marsden, D. (1973), *Mothers Alone: Poverty and the fatherless family*, Harmondsworth: Penguin.

Martin, J. and Roberts, C. (1984), *Women and Employment: A lifetime's perspective*, London: HMSO.

Matteson, D. (1985), 'Bisexual men in marriage: Is a positive homosexual identity and stable marriage possible?', in F. Klein and T. Wolf (eds), *Bisexualities: Theory and research*, New York: Haworth.

Melhuishe, E. and Moss, P. (eds) (1991), *Day Care for Young Children: International perspective*, London: Routledge.

Meulders-Klein, M. and Eekelaar, J. (eds) (1988), *Family, State and Individual Economic Security*, Brussels: Story Scientia.

Millar, J. (1987), 'Lone mothers', in C. Glendinning and J. Millar (eds), *Women and Poverty in Britain*, Hemel Hempstead: Harvester Wheatsheaf.

Millar, J. (1988), 'The costs of marital breakdown', in R. Walker and G. Parker (eds), *Money Matters: Income, wealth and financial welfare*, London: Sage.

Millar, J. (1989), *Poverty and the Lone-parent Family: The challenge to social policy*, Aldershot: Gower.

Millar, J., Cooke, K. and McLaughlin, E. (1989), 'The employment lottery: Risk and social security benefits', *Policy and Politics*, **17**, 1: 75–81.

Miller, B. (1979), 'Gay fathers and their children', *Family Co-ordinator*, **28**: 544–52.

Mills, C.W. (1970), *The Sociological Imagination*, Harmondsworth: Penguin.

Mills, C.W. (1972), 'Situated actions and vocabularies of

motives', in J. Manis and B. Meltzer (eds), *Symbolic Interaction: A reader in social psychology*, 2nd edn, Boston: Allyn & Bacon.

Mills, T. (1985), 'The assault on the self: Stages in coping with battering husbands', *Qualitative Sociology*, **8**: 103–23.

Mitchell, J. (1975), *Psychoanalysis and Feminism*, Harmondsworth: Penguin.

Mitton, R. and Willmott, R. (1983), *Unemployment, Poverty and Social Policy in Europe*, London: Bedford Square Press.

Morgan, D. (1985), *The Family, Politics and Social Theory*, London: Routledge & Kegan Paul.

Morris, J. and Winn, M. (1990), *Housing and Social Inequality*, London: Hilary Shipman.

Morris, L. (1990), *The Workings of the Household: A US–UK comparison*, Cambridge: Polity Press.

Morrison, D. and Henkel, R. (eds) (1970), *The Significance Test Controversy*, Chicago: Aldine.

Mullan, B. (1984), *The Mating Trade*, London: Routledge & Kegan Paul.

Murgatroyd, S. and Woolfe, R. (1982), *Coping with Crisis*, London: Harper & Row.

Murie, A. (1983), *Housing Inequality and Deprivation*, London: Heinemann.

Murie, A. (1986), 'Social deprivation in urban areas: Housing inequality or occupational class at work?', *Tijdschriltvoor Economische En Sociale Geografie*, **77**: 345–57.

Murphy, M. (1989), 'Housing the people: From shortage to surplus?', in H. Joshi (ed.), *The Changing Population of Britain*, Oxford: Basil Blackwell.

Nissel, M. (1987), 'Social change and the family cycle', in G. Cohen (ed.), *Social Change and the Life Course*, London: Tavistock.

Nixon, J. (1979), *Fatherless Families on Family Income Supplement*, DHSS Research Paper No. 4, London: HMSO.

Oakley, A. (1974), *Housewife*, Harmondsworth: Penguin.

O'Brien, M. (1987), 'Kinship and friendship among lone fathers', in C. Lewis and M. O'Brien (eds), *Reassessing Fatherhood*, London: Sage.

Office of Population Censuses and Surveys (1980), *General Household Survey*, London: HMSO.

Office of Population Censuses and Surveys (1981), *General Household Survey*, London: HMSO.

Office of Population Censuses and Surveys (1982), *General Household Survey*, London: HMSO.

O'Higgins, M. (1987), *Lone Parent Families in the European Community: Numbers and socio-economic characteristics*, Bath: University of Bath.

O'Higgins, M., Bradshaw, J. and Walker, R. (1988), 'Income distribution over the life cycle', in R. Walker and G. Parker (eds), *Money Matters: Money, wealth and financial welfare*, London: Sage.

Oppenheim, C. (1990), *Poverty: The facts*, London: Child Poverty Action Group.

Page, R. (1984), *Stigma*, London: Routledge & Kegan Paul.

Pahl, J. (1985), 'Violent husbands and abused wives: A longitudinal study', in J. Pahl (ed.), *Private Violence and Public Policy: The needs of battered women and the response of the public services*, London: Routledge & Kegan Paul.

Pahl, J. (1989), *Money and Marriage*, London and Basingstoke: Macmillan.

Pahl, R.E. (1984), *Divisions of Labour*, Oxford: Basil Blackwell.

Papernow, P. (1984), 'Stepfamily cycle', *Family Relations*, **33**: 355–63.

Parish, T. and Kappes, B. (1980), 'Impact of father loss on the family', *Social Behaviour and Personality*, **8**: 107–12.

Pascall, G. (1986), *Social Policy: A feminist analysis*, London: Tavistock.

Pascaud, E. and Simenon, B. (1987), 'Pauvreté et précarité, *Données Sociales*, Paris: Institut National de la Statistique et des Etudes Economiques.

Pasley, K. (1987), 'Family boundary ambiguity: Perceptions of adult step-family members', in K. Pasley and M. Ihinger-Tallman (eds), *Remarriage and Stepparenting: Current research and theory*, New York: Guilford Press.

Petrie, P. and Logan, P. (1986), *After School and in the Holidays: The responsibility for looking after children*, Thomas Coram Research Unit, Working and Occasional Papers 2, London.

Phillips, A. (1989), 'Action re Play', *The Guardian*, 6 December.

Phillips, R. (1988), *Putting Asunder: A history of divorce in western society*, Cambridge: Cambridge University Press.

Phoenix, A. (1991), *Young Mothers?*, Cambridge: Polity Press.

Pill, C.J. (1990), 'Stepfamilies: Redefining the family', *Family Relations*, **39**: 186–93.

Platt, S., Martin, C., Hunt, S. and Lewis, C. (1989), 'Damp housing, mould growth and symptomatic health state', *British Medical Journal*, **298**: 1673–8.

Plummer, K. (1975), *Sexual Stigma*, London: Routledge & Kegan Paul.

Popay, J. and Jones, G. (1988), 'Explaining the sting in the tail: Social role theories and gender inequalities in health', paper presented to Social Policy Association Conference, Edinburgh.

Popay, J. and Jones, G. (1990), 'Patterns of health and illness amongst lone parents', *Journal of Social Policy*, **19**, 4: 499–534.

Popay, J., Rimmer, L. and Rossiter, L. (1983), *One Parent Families: Parents, children and public policy*, London: Study Commission on the Family, Paper No. 12.

Qureshi, H. and Simons, K. (1987), 'Resources within families: Caring for elderly people', in J. Brannen and G. Wilson (eds), *Give and Take in Families*, London: Allen & Unwin.

Rallu, J.L. (1982a), 'Les Effets des nouveaux rythmes', *Les Familles d'aujourd'hui*, No. 2.

Rallu, J.L. (1982b), 'Les Enfants des familles monoparentales', *Population*, **37** (1): 51–74.

Reissman, C. and Gerstel, N. (1985), 'Marital dissolution and health: Do males or females have greater risk?' *Social Science and Medicine*, **20**, 6: 627–35.

Renvoize, J. (1985), *Going Solo: Single mothers by choice*, London: Routledge & Kegan Paul.

Rich, A. (1980), 'Compulsory heterosexuality and lesbian existence', *Signs: Journal of Women and Culture in Society*, **5**: 631–60.

Richards, L.N. (1989), 'The precarious survival and hard-won satisfactions of white single-parent families', *Family Relations*, **38**: 396–403.

Richards, M. and Light, P. (eds) (1986), *Children of Social Worlds*, Cambridge: Polity Press.

Richards, M.P.M. and Dyson, M. (1982), *Separation, Divorce and the Development of Children: A report*, unpublished, London: DHSS.

Richman, N. (1978), 'Depression in mothers of young children', *Journal of the Royal Society of Medicine*, **71**: 489–93.

Riley, D. (1983), *War in the Nursery: Theories of the child and mother*, London: Virago.

Rimmer, L. (1983), 'Changing Family Patterns', in A.W. Franklin (ed.), *Family Matters: Perspectives on the family and social policy*, Oxford: Pergamon Press.

Roll, J. (1989), *Lone Parent Families in the European Community*, London: Family Policy Studies Centre.

Rose, H. (1985), 'Women's refuges: Creating new forms of welfare?', in C. Ungerson (ed.), *Women and Social Policy: A reader*, London and Basingstoke: Macmillan.

Ross, M. (1983), *The Married Homosexual Man: A psychological study*, London: Routledge & Kegan Paul.

Rubington, E. and Weinberg, M. (eds) (1987), *Deviance: The interactionist perspective*, New York: Macmillan.

Sardanis-Zimmerman, I. (1977), *The Stepmother: Mythology and self-perception*, unpublished dissertation, California School of Professional Psychology.

Sarre, P., Phillips, D. and Skellington, R. (1989), *Ethnic Minority Housing: Explanations and policies*, Aldershot: Avebury.

Sauvy, A. (1969), *General Theory of Population*, London: Weidenfeld & Nicolson.

Schulman, G.L. (1972), 'Myths that intrude on the adaptation of the stepfamily', *Social Casework*, **49**: 131–9.

Scott, M. and Lyman, S. (1968), 'Accounts', *American Sociological Review*, **33**: 46–62.

Scully, D. and Marolla, J. (1984), 'Convicted rapists' excuses and justifications', *Social Problems*, **31**: 530–44.

Seel, R. (1987), *The Uncertain Father*, Bath: Gateway Books.

Segalman, R. and Marsland, D. (1989), *Cradle to Grave*, London and Basingstoke: Macmillan.

Sharpe, S. (1984), *Double Identity: The lives of working mothers*, Harmondsworth: Penguin.

Simon, A.W. (1964), *Stepchild in the Family: A view of children in remarriage*, New York: Odyssey Press.

Simon, J.L. (1983), 'The present value of population growth in the western world', *Population Studies*, **37**, 1: 5–21.

Simpson, R. (1978), *Daycare for School-Age Children*, Manchester: Equal Opportunities Commission.

Slipman, S. and Hadjipateras, A. (1988), *Helping One-Parent Families to Work*, London: National Council for One Parent Families.

Smart, C. (1984), *The Ties that Bind: Law, marriage and the reproduction of patriarchal relations*, London: Routledge & Kegan Paul.

Smeeding, T.M., O'Higgins, M. and Rainwater, L. (1990), *Poverty, Inequality and Income Distribution in Comparative Perspectives*, Hemel Hempstead: Harvester Wheatsheaf.

Squires, P. (1990), *Anti-Social Policy: Welfare, ideology and the disciplinary state*, Hemel Hempstead: Harvester Wheatsheaf.

Stern, P. (1978), 'Stepfamilies: Integration around child discipline issues', *Mental Health Nursing*, 1: 49–56.

Sullivan, O. (1986), 'Housing movements of the divorced and separated', *Housing Studies*, 1: 35–48.

Sykes, G. and Matza, D. (1957), 'Techniques of neutralization: A theory of delinquency', *American Sociological Review*, 22: 664–70.

Taffin, C. (1987), 'La Mobilité résidentielle entre 1979 et 1984', in *Données Sociales*, Paris: Institut National de la Statistique et des Etudes Economiques.

Thornes, B. and Collard, J. (1979), *Who Divorces?*, London: Routledge and Kegan Paul.

Tivers, J. (1985), *Women Attached: The daily lives of women with young children*, London: Croom Helm.

Todd, E. (1988), *The Explanation of Ideology: Family structures and social systems*, Oxford: Basil Blackwell.

Took, L. and Ford, J. (1987), 'The impact of mortgage arrears on the housing careers of home owners', in A. Bryman, B. Bytheway, P. Allatt and T. Keil (eds), *Rethinking the Life Cycle*, London and Basingstoke: Macmillan.

Townsend, P. (1979), *Poverty in the United Kingdom: A survey of household resources and standards of living*, Harmondsworth: Penguin.

Townsend, P. with Corrigan, P. and Kowarzik, U. (1987), *Poverty and Labour in London*, London: Low Pay Unit.

Troiden, R. (1988), *Gay and Lesbian Identity*, New York: General Hall.

Vaughan, D. (1986), *Uncoupling: Turning points in intimate relationships*, Oxford: Oxford University Press.

Verbrugge, L. (1989), 'The twain meet: Empirical explanations of sex differences in health and mortality', *Journal of Health and Social Behaviour*, 30: 232–304.

Verdier, P. (1984), *Mémento d'Aide Sociale*, Paris: ESF.

Villac, M. (1984), 'Les Familles monoparentales', in *Données Sociales*, Institut National de la Statistique et des Etudes Economiques.

Visher, E.B. and Visher, J.S. (1979), *Stepfamilies: A guide to working with stepparents and stepchildren*, New York: Brunner/Mazel.

Voysey, M. (1975), *A Constant Burden: The reconstitution of family life*, London: Routledge & Kegan Paul.

Walker, A. and Walker, C. (eds) (1987), *The Growing Divide: A social audit 1979–1987*, London: Child Poverty Action Group.

Walker, R. (1988), 'The costs of household formation', in R. Walker and G. Parker (eds), *Money Matters: Money, wealth and financial welfare*, London: Sage.

Wallerstein, J.S. (1984), 'Children of divorce: Preliminary report of a ten-year follow-up of young children', *American Journal of Orthopsychiatry*, **54**: 444–58.

Wallerstein, J.S. and Kelly, J. (1980), *Surviving the Break-up*, London: Grant Macintyre.

Wallman, S. (1984), *Eight London Households*, London: Tavistock.

Watson, S. (1987), 'Ideas of the family in the development of housing form', in M. Loney *et al.* (eds), *The State of the Market: Politics and welfare in contemporary Britain*, London: Sage.

Watson, S. (1988), *Accommodating Inequality: Gender and housing*, Sydney: Allen & Unwin.

Watson, S. with Austerberry, H. (1986), *Housing and Homelessness: A feminist perspective*, London: Routledge & Kegan Paul.

Weale, A., Bradshaw, J., Maynard, A. and Piachaud, D. (1984), *Lone Parents, Paid Work and Social Security*, London: Occasional Papers on Social Administration 77, National Council for Voluntary Organizations.

Weeks, J. (1986), *Sexuality*, Chichester: Ellis Horwood.

West, D.J. (1982), *Delinquency: Its roots, careers and prospects*, London: Heinemann.

West, D.J. and Farrington, D.P. (1973), *Who Becomes Delinquent?*, London: Heinemann.

White, L.K. and Booth, A. (1985), 'The quality and stability of remarriages: The role of children', *American Sociological Review*, **50**: 689–98.

Whiteley, P.F. and Winyard, S.J. (1987), *Pressure for the poor: The poverty lobby and policy making*, London: Methuen.

Whiteside, M.F. (1989), 'Family rituals as a key to kinship

connections in remarried families', *Family Relations*, **38**: 34–9.

Wicks, M. (1983), 'Does Britain need a family policy?', in A.W. Franklin (ed.), *Family Matters: Perspectives on the family and social policy*, Oxford: Pergamon Press.

Williams, F. (1989), *Social Policy: A critical introduction*, Cambridge: Polity Press.

Willmott, P. and Murie, A. (1988), *Polarisation and Social Housing: The British and French experience*, London: Policy Studies Institute.

Wilson, K.L., Zurcher, L.A., MacAdams, D.C. and Curtis, R.L. (1975), 'Stepfathers and stepchildren: An exploratory analysis from two national surveys', *Journal of Marriage and the Family*, **37**: 526–36.

Wimbush, E. (1986), *Women, Leisure and Well-Being*, Edinburgh: Centre for Leisure Research.

Yeandle, S. (1984), *Women's Working Lives: Patterns and strategies*, London: Tavistock.

Yudkin, S. and Holme, A. (1963), *Working Mothers and Their Children*, London: Michael Joseph.

Zick, C.D. and Smith, K.R. (1988), 'Recent widowhood, remarriage and changes in economic well-being', *Journal of Marriage and the Family*, **50**: 233–44.

Index